Other titles of interest from IPI Press

The Will of the Unseen *Hans Lynge*
Ivalu's Color *Nauja Lynge*
Journal in Greenland *Hans Egede Saabye*
Inuit Folk-tales *Knud Rasmussen*
Vikings of Today *Wilfred Grenfell*
Tales of Yukaghir *Waldemar Bogoras*
Eden of the North *Signe Rink*
The Diary of Johannes Hansen
Singnagtugaq *Mathias Storch*
Inuit Poems and Tales *collected by William Thalbitzer*
Tuumarsi *Fredrik Nielsen*
Kayakmen *collected by Signe Rink*
The Veins of the Heart to the Pinnacle of the Mind *Aqqaluk Lynge*

The Right to a Father

The Right to a Father

The Letters of Anne Sofie Hardenberg

Annotated by Pia Christensen Bang
Translated from Danish by Susan Stanley

IPI

Distributed by University Press of New England
upne.com

Translated from Danish
Kampen for en far

Funded in part by a grant from
DANISH ARTS FOUNDATION
Copenhagen, Denmark

First English edition

ISBN 978-0-9967480-3-2

IPI Press
Post Office Box 212
Hanover, New Hampshire 03755
email: ipolari@gmail.com

Contents

Foreword
By Jørgen Fleischer

This book in hand is a very interesting correspondence between a Greenlandic girl and her Danish family.

In the years of rebuilding after the war, many young Danish men travelled to Greenland and developed relationships with young Greenlandic girls. During the cultural clash, it was often the case that such relationships failed and the Greenlandic girl was left alone with a child which was then raised by the grandparents.

This was also the case for Anne Sofie. The engagement between her Greenlandic mother, Helene Isaksen, and her father, the Dane Svend Weber, who was the engineer in Prince Christians Sound, was broken off.

Fatherless children were nothing new in Greenlandic society. In the early days of the fisheries, many men died at sea. Grandparents raising their grandchildren was not new, either. Earlier, when three generations lived in the same house in just one single room, the grandparents had great impact in the raising of children, and back then, fatherless children were not bullied by their friends. The child could not help that their father was dead.

But it was a different matter with pre-marital children of Danish fathers and Greenlandic mothers. Anne Sofie's father was alive but his daughter was not living with him–she did not even know where he was.

She endured much hardship as a child. She grew up in modest conditions and her school mates bullied and teased her because she was fatherless. It hurt her a lot and as an adolescent, she decided to find her Danish father, slightly against her mother's will. She managed to get in touch with him in Denmark and he received her well but his wife did not; she worked against Anne Sofie's entrance into the family. Her paternal aunt, however, and gradually her half-brother, too, received her warmly and corresponded with her. It is this correspondence that is the focal point of this book.

The many letters document a specific era–its norms and values–as well as the feelings involved from all sides involved in Anne Sofie's brave insistence to have a relationship to her father and family in Denmark.

It was not only Svend Weber's Danish wife who was opposed to Anne Sofie reaching out to her Danish family. Her mother, Helene Isaksen, was also very much against it, and for many years there was no warmth in the relationship between mother and daughter either.

Only many years later did Anne Sofie achieve peace in relationship to her mother. At her mother's 75th birthday, she calls her "mother" for the first time and gives a speech on forgiveness and love.

Anne Sofie's oldest son is named after her grandfather, Svend.

Today, Anne Sofie, nee Hardenberg, is a notable ambassador for Greenland in the culinary field.

◉ Prince Christian Sound
September 4, 1947

Asasara atât!

I have received three letters from you at the same time and a lovely picture. Thank you for it all.

I long for you, too, and think of you often, and wonder whether you are doing well in Denmark. When are you are coming back up here again, I do not really know, perhaps sometime in 1948? I am in the process of applying for another position from the board so we can get married and then stay up here for a number of years, but it will probably not happen until the fall of '48 as my contract is for 2 years. I can remain at Prince Christian but we are not allowed to have our wives here as the station is so far removed. I would like to know what you are doing at Mother and Father's place? Are you learning to cook? I have written to Father that you will be going to vocational school.

In June, I was on vacation in Nanortalik for 3 weeks, I stayed with Dr. Rendal and had a wonderful time, but I missed you a lot.

(1st page of letter from Svend Weber to Helene Isaksen)

It is August 28, 1948. A little girl is born in Qaqortoq. The mother is Helene Isaksen, a young woman who has returned to her hometown to live with her parents and her many siblings and lick her wounds from a broken engagement.

A few years before, Helene met the Danish engineer Svend Weber, who works at the meteorology station at Prince Christian Sound in South Greenland. The young couple is madly in love and plan to get married, but it is not allowed to have wives or girlfriends so instead, Helene travels to Denmark to live with Svend's parents and to learn more about cooking, housekeeping, and Danish society until the dream of a shared life can become a reality.

An ardent correspondence keeps the love alive and when Helene travels back to Greenland after her stay with her in-laws to be, she briefly meets with Svend who still has to take his employment contract into consideration. Nevertheless, Helene becomes pregnant but something goes wrong in their relationship. The engagement is broken off and Helene is alone when she gives birth to her daughter. The little girl is christened Anne Sofie.

As Anne Sofie grows up, she becomes more and more aware of her missing father. She is told early on that her father is Danish, that his name is Svend, and that he is an engineer but apart from that, there is only a distant uncle who occasionally tells the girl a little about her father. Neither Anne Sofie, Helene, nor anyone else is in contact with him. When she plays with her girlfriends and visits them, she often feels a stab to her heart. She does not have a family like that. She does not have a father at home. For many years, Helene, too, is thousands of kilometers away. When Anne Sofie is two years old, both her mother and several of her siblings are infected with tuberculosis and they travel to Denmark to recover from the disease in a sanitarium. Helene's stay is prolonged, the disease will not let go of her, and her health is unable to withstand the Greenlandic cold, so it is several years before she returns to her daughter. Anne Sofie has started school when her mother finally returns home and the absence of both parents in her early childhood leaves its mark on her. She becomes a quiet and introverted girl who does not wish to attract attention and risk her playmates' scornful remarks about not having a father. She never lacks love from her maternal grandmother with whom she lives, but there is not a lot of money. Most often she gets hand-me-downs from her mother's siblings; sometimes she has to stay indoors and play because there are no clothes for her. She often dreams about all the things that would be different if only she had a "real" family and a father that made money.

There is lively air traffic then, as it is during the Korean War. American planes are flying to and from the military base in Narsarsuaq and Anne Sofie imagines her father might be sitting up in one of the planes as a pilot, waving down to her. She knows he is an engineer but engineers do so many exciting things, so you never know... It happens that she cautiously asks her mother about her father, but that does not get her anywhere. Helene absolutely refuses to talk about Svend so Anne Sofie will have to settle for dreaming, and she dreams a lot.

While Anne Sofie's maternal grandmother has always taken care of her and raised her as one of her own children, it is very obvious that some of her mother's siblings find that the little girl is mostly just an extra mouth to feed and, at times, an unwanted foster child. They talk badly about Helene, the broken engagement, and the girl whom she has now placed with her mother. Anne Sofie hears many comments about her disappeared father and feels different – outside the community. She does not have her mother's black hair and dark eyes, but is much lighter than the rest of the family. She feels that they are pointing their fingers at her and use any occasion to emphasize that she is worthless.

When Anne Sofie gets confirmed, she would like to have the party with her cousin of the same age, and in spite of her mother's warnings, that is the way it is. Helene is afraid that the family will get drunk and again use the occasion to expose her and her daughter. When the big day comes and all the guests arrive, Anne Sofie and her mother are placed at a small table away from the horse-shoe setup at which the other guests are sitting. That way everyone can see the family's weirdos, the cousin's mother and stepfather – who are already drunk.

Anne Sofie does not remember much else from her confirmation other than crying and crying.

When Anne Sofie as an adolescent gets in close contact with one of her aunts, she describes in several letters how she perceived her childhood:

◉ Nuuk
September 2, 1967

Dear Ruth,

Thank you for your long letter which I received two weeks ago – I apologize for not responding immediately as you requested. I was quite surprised by the harsh tone of the letter, it is the second time in my life I had such a letter. Oh well, it is bound to happen someday and now it has happened again. But one learns from one's own mistakes.

You wrote that I let you down that last day – I will never let you down in any way, Aunt. I left that morning because I had to, because there were several important things I had to take care of before I travelled home. I can tell you, Ruth, the last week I spent with you, I felt trapped in a cage and when you said that you would rather I not go to Arne. You were so scared and frightened that I would get pregnant or that anything at all would go wrong. I could feel it when you spoke to me. So I tell you, I am 19 years old, not 15 – I know what I am doing.

Aunt Ruth, I do not only think about myself, I do not, perhaps you had that impression of me. Ruth, I am very sorry that I had completely forgotten the money I owed you – it is truly strange, that you did not remind me – you know I had money and you could have had it right away. You will get that money back, I would like to send it to Denmark but, of course, I do not know what to do about it, and tell me how much I owe you – so I can be done with hearing more about it. Furthermore, if you feel cheated from the trip to France, or rather, all the time I have been staying with you, you can have all the money back you spent on me.You can easily get it back if you wish. If you at all feel cheated by me, feel free to break the relation between us, but of course I do not wish it as I do not want to lose you, my only faithful Aunt.

Ruth, you cannot demand that I refrain from speaking Greenlandic in my everyday life, you know so little about Greenland that I can even feel it in the way you speak. One cannot refrain from speaking it even if one tries. Up here, Greenlanders become all frazzled when they hear a native speak Danish to someone who is a Greenlander. It is wrong, but that is how it is here. Ruth, a person should be able to decide which kind of magazine or book to read, it is one's own private matter. Of course it is wrong to read the empty weekly magazines full of sex, but one does it anyway.

I think you demand too much of me at once, I cannot do it all at the same time, but it will happen gradually. Similarly, one should not demand too much of one person at one time, that too will be difficult – and remember, I have an entirely different background than the Danes – raised in a completely different way and have experienced a lot from my own childhood.You do not know my life at all, I have endured much, both good and bad.

When I was a child, my mother was in Denmark for the most part of the first eight years – I lived with my Grandmother among many of my mother's siblings and there were bad family circumstances.When I was little, I could not go outside because I had no clothes and when I was an infant, I cried all the time because there was no milk for me and my mothers brother used to console me, but he cried because he felt so bad for me for not having any milk. They used to get another lady to nurse me, that way I managed. My mother's family did not like me, I was always pushed aside when some festivity took place. Throughout my entire childhood I have been pushed aside, until I was confirmed. When my mother returned home in 1956, we were hated and pushed aside because we lived with my grandmother and my mother's siblings hated her. At her workplace she was hated and there were always bad rumors and they were all blamed on me. At my confirmation, my mother and I were hated by the entire family and were pushed aside so that the guests could see how wretched we were – it was the worst thing I have experienced in my life, my confirmation. After my confirmation in 8th and 9th grade, there were bad rumors and lies about me around the town and children at school threw rocks at me. When they saw me they chased me and yelled lies at me. I lost my friends and girlfriends. Everyone hated me and no one wanted to believe me. I would hide so no one could see me. All those rumors were lies.

You were right, Aunt Ruth, I was never happy, never said anything. Throughout my childhood, I have always kept my words to myself, I kept them inside. I had no one I could tell. I was very introverted. I almost fled from people, I went for walks alone at night, skied alone in the mountains in the dark, considered suicide. I have had inferiority complexes, I felt discouraged by other people even though I know they are not worth more than I am. I am still that way – I feel I am worth less than others, I feel they look down on me. I have the same feeling now with my two best girlfriends Magga and Karen Marie, I ended our friendships because I felt worthless. Those two always spoke about their good family relations, about their fathers, mothers, and siblings, how well they were and what they had, and I thought that since I do not have either of these things, I had nothing to say. I felt like I was worthless. I am sad because I am this way, perhaps I will open up over time. I am never happy now, either, except for when I receive a letter from Arne. I am always quiet and calm.

Ruth, two weeks ago I received my lost Christmas present from you. It was Mr. Holm from the the Printing House who had found the parcel floating in the harbor.The content is undamaged and the bathrobe and the wooden candleholder are intact. I am very happy for the housecoat, it is very pretty and cute, it fits me very well. Its actually amazing that it can float for that long in the water, I think it is the plastic bag that has kept it afloat. I shall write to Bent, too, and thank him.

I am actually well up here.We have had a bit of snow outside and it is cold, especially when there is barely any hair on one's head (I have cut my hair short). My mother is doing rather well, she has become very lively and her friend is very nice, engineer Randrup, he has a private engineering company up here.

Aunt Ruth, what should I do, can I get my father's name rather easily? Am I not supposed to report to the church first? I would like to have father's name. I do not yet have the document regarding the inheritance, I dared not ask her for it. I feel bad for her, but I guess I will someday.

The most loving greetings
from Anne Sofie

◎ Nuuk
October 29, 1967

Dear Aunt Ruth,

Many thanks for your lovely letter. I was very relieved when I had finished it. Tears of joy were shed, it is as if there was new hope for me. I am happy to hear that you were happy to hear about what I have experienced in my young life. Yes, it has been difficult, it still is. I still encounter opposition from my mother's family and from mother, they usually express that they do not like my beloved Arne. Last Friday I walked home, sobbing from insult, I could not do anything else. It was my mother who said that she does not like my love at all. In the afternoon my mother's sisters husband told me that they had just been quarreling about Arne, one did not want me to see Arne. It goes on like this until we perhaps get married. I do not think my mother will become friends with him.

Aunt Ruth, I was actually happy to live with you, it was just that I was too reserved – I actually had quite a lot to tell you about my childhood. Now I have realized that I have not yet gotten beyond being introverted or from my inferiority complexes, it is worst now, at this moment. I feel less self worth than other people and friends. It is perhaps due to my longing for Arne, I miss him terribly much. He is doing pretty well, but he wrote that his knee has been a torment for him lately. He did not even want to see the doctor – he wrote that it is no use, it will interrupt his school time, and his examination is not far off. He wrote that they had been tested in operating technique, 50 questions in 4 hours and he received top marks along with someone called Marianne. I am afraid that he will end up being unable to walk with that knee, it is getting worse, I remember how much pain he has been in while I have known him. There is nothing I can do.

Aunt Ruth, I received the slides a month ago. They turned out really good considering it was the first time I have taken color images. The picture with Mikkeline from Løkken next to her car is really good as is the one of Michäel. Aunt Grethe wrote that Arne has shown his slides from Greenland as well as the ones that he took in Odense. She wrote that they are good. You see, I had written to Arne that he should show them to her and Bent was there too. I have just written to Bent to thank him for the lost Christmas presents that suddenly showed up.

Yes, we did get a little snow but it is quite little. I look forward to real snow – then I can enjoy my skiing trips. You are lucky, you are in the warmth. It is very cold up here in the High North. Grandmother is coming back home this November, she has grown tired of Denmark. Or rather, I think, she has become very disappointed with Kasper, Karl, and Olivie, they are not doing well. I have not heard from them since I was with them. My mother was supposed to travel to Qaqortoq to see her but she told me today that she will not be traveling after all. She is probably scared of leaving Doctor Joensen. She started seeing him (a Faroese) down at the outpatient clinic. She left Randrup who is a private engineer, poor man. He is so sad because mother left him, for he is very kind, that Randrup. Doctor Joensen is also very kind, now and then I am invited to dinner with them, they have a good time together. I hope it lasts.

I shall write to Ellen Margrethe like you asked me. I talked a bit with mother about the inheritance. She said that she had received some kind of document that she had to fill out in October 1966 and she had sent it back immediately. She said that it did not mention how much it was, only that it was something she had to fill out. She told me that it was something father had written in 1956 to say that if he had a child in Greenland, she was to have some of the inheritance and that the document had not been renewed.

Aunt Ruth, do not worry at all about any gift, I have received more than enough from you. I can tell you that I care more about you than my mother. I miss you when I worry, you see, I have no one to turn to when my love is far away but he will be back in 7 weeks, and those 7 weeks are nothing.

Aunt Ruth, I see Arne's parents at the school every day, his mother is there every day for 2 hours to help Peter with the toilet, she is always good at smiling and greeting me. I have not visited them yet, though I had expected them to invite me, but it will happen someday.

Yes, it is exciting to see where I will be working as a maid. I spoke with my Mother's girlfriend about her knowing a doctor's family that had small children and would like a young maid in their house. She told me that they lived in Esrum a little outside Odense. She said she would write to them. It would be rather nice to be close by grandmother, I would prefer that. I want to be with her as long as I have her. My mother also knows a doctor's family in Odense with small children. She said she would try them if the girlfriend could not help me. Apart from that, I am waiting for a reply from Mrs. Varning whom I wrote to long ago.

I will stop for now. I send you all greetings from Greenland.

The most loving greetings from your devoted Anne Sofie

The history prior to confiding in Aunt Ruth is rather dramatic.

When she is 15 years old, Anne Sofie moves from Qaqortoq to Nuuk to go to secondary school. Here, she lives some distance away from her mother with whom her relationship has gradually become rather strained. Instead she becomes closely attached to her girlfriends from school who also live in the dormitory with her. Several of her friends are in the same situation as Anne Sofie, either they have never known their father or that he, early in their lives, has disappeared out of the children's lives. Many Danish men have worked in Greenland for a shorter or longer period of time and gotten to know Greenlandic women, and even so well that it often resulted in children. Many of them, however, refrain from searching for them or contacting their lost fathers – either because their mothers do not know where the men have gone or out of fear of being rejected.

In 1964, the *Grønlandsmesterskaber* (Greenlandic Championship) in soccer takes place in Nuuk and Anne Sofie's girlfriend from school, Lotte from Maniitsoq, spends the occasion searching for her father whom she has never met even though she knows that he, too, lives in Nuuk. Lotte has a woman from Maniitsoq visiting who knows how her father looks and who helps her look for him in the big crowds at the soccer matches. Lotte is able to find out who he is and bravely introduces herself to him. Lotte's father is happy to have been found by his daughter and immediately they have a warm and close relationship.

The girlfriend's success whetted Anne Sofie's appetite. She is not afraid of resistance, her wish to find her father is growing stronger and stronger. She wants to find him, no matter what. She knows that her mother has lived with her father's parents to learn Danish housekeeping and she asks Helene for her grandmother's address. Helene's first reaction is pure rejection and anger. Why does Anne Sofie have to go digging into that old matter, there is no reason for that and no good will come of it. But Anne Sofie insists and finally gets the address from her mother.

She writes a letter to the grandmother, Hedvig Nielsen in Odense, tells her who she is and explains that she would like to get in contact with her father and get to know him. After a couple of weeks of excited waiting, Anne Sofie receives a letter. It is a letter from her father. A letter, which has later disappeared, where Svend Weber thanks his daughter very much for her initiative. He would very much like to get to know her and is happy that they now have found each other. In his letter, he tells her that he has married Britta and that they have two children together, Per and Annette. Suddenly, Anne Sofie has a father, a step mother, and two half siblings. She writes to her father that she is going to Denmark for school for three months the following summer, in 1966. And she receives an answer that Svend would very much like to meet her and introduce her to his family.

◉ Copenhagen
March 15, 1966

Dear Anne Sofie,

Thank you so much for your letter from 1.14.66. It arrived just in time for my birthday on January 19. This year I turned 45 so it is an old father you have although I do not feel it. It makes sense that many thoughts appear and now I will tell you a little bit about your family in Denmark.

My mother turned 75 in 1965, we celebrated this day in our home in J. E. Ohlsens Gade. My mother is in good health, although she suffers from arthritis, but she takes care of herself and lives in Odense. My father passed away in the Christmas of 1959 after several years of illness, I suspect it was some kind of calcification which is a quite normal age-related illness. As you may know, my father was a traveling salesman.

We are four children: Knud who is 50 years old, educated in sales, later a police officer, also in Greenland, ¾ year in Holsteinberg. Now he is a consultant in the Ministry of Social Affairs. My sister Ruth, 48 years old, trained as a nurse, later traveled abroad, most recently 2 years in India (center for leprosy), has been home for 1 year but is soon going to India again.

Bent, my younger brother, is married to an English girl, has 2 children, and is still living in England but is moving to Denmark this coming summer. He is 33 years old. And finally there is your father: trained engineer, 1945-51 Greenland, 1951-55 Copenhagen's Public Transportation, superintendent for the bus department, 1955-56 (1½ year) superintendent in the lead mine of Mestersvig, 1957-58 super-intendent in Turkey where the family joined me. 1958-59 super-

intendent in Kangerlussuaq for the mechanical repair shops for D.A.G. 1959-? Employed as industrial engineer at the Byggeriets Maskinstationer A/S (Agricultural Construction Contractor Inc.). This company rents out machines to contractors building housing and factories. We have approximately 200 employees, a fine job that enables me to travel in the Netherlands, Belgium, Germany, England, and Sweden. In my last letter I told you about my trip to Thorshavn. In this coming week I am going to London for 5 days to talk to our suppliers.

My wife's name is Britta. In the summer she and the children live in a small house on Bornholm by Ypnasted, which is an old fishing village and right by the sea, we bought it a few years ago, and we spend all our vacations there: Easter, Pentecost, summer break, fall break, and in 1965 Christmas too. Other than that there is a lot to do here in Copenhagen between approximately 9 AM and 6 PM. I drive a lot, approximately 4000 km each month, when I visit customers and lead the work.

That was a bit about what is going on down here and how we live. You must have patience in regards to the pictures, they are coming. I will very much like to hear from you.

The most loving greetings,
Svend

Anne Sofie is delighted and beamingly tells her girlfriends, classmates and mother about the new contact. After months of impatient waiting and fervent correspondence across the Atlantic between father and daughter, the time when the class goes to Denmark finally arrives. Anne Sofie is excited and both her friends and teachers pay close attention to each contact and hope that they, too, will be able to meet their girlfriend's "new" father.

June 19, 1966

Dear Anne Sofie!

Welcome to Denmark. Unfortunately it turned out that I was in Fredericia the day you arrived (Tuesday morning) and Ruth has gone to Italy for a 10 day vacation. We look forward to meeting you. From Thursday June 23rd I am in Kolding, phone xxx-xxxx, through July 15th. Address: Byggeriets Maskinstationer A/S, Agtrupvej xxx, Kolding.

Tuesday morning on the 21st, Britta, Per, and Annette are going on summer vacation to Bornholm where we have a small house. They return from Bornholm around August 10, I myself am going to Bornholm July 27-August 10.

But we shall see when we are able to meet, it should not have to be too long.

The most loving greetings,
Svend

Attached:

Closer, God, to you,
Closer to you!
Is it than the road of the cross,
You show me
Always, however, I sing:
Closer, God, to you,
Closer to you
Whether late in the hour of sorrow
Lonely I go
And have for bed only
The rock so hard,
The dream, however, carries me
Closer, God, to you
Closer to you
Here is, with the hope of heaven
Betel for me:
The rocks in baptismal tears
I anoint you,
Dauntless goes on my way
Closer, God, to you,
Closer to you
And is for the last time
The battle over
The soul to heaven-meadow
Lifting itself free.
Forever, then, I cheer
Home, my God, with you
Home with you.

The young Greenlanders are housed at Elsinore Hostel on June 15, from here they will go on a lot of day trips and visits all around to better get to know Danish society as well as attending a Danish school for a period. They visit Tivoli Gardens, the Botanic Garden, Copenhagen Zoo, and many other places. While they are in the Tivoli Gardens, Anne Sofie plucked up courage and for the first time she calls her father on his private phone. After a few days where she speaks with him on the phone several times, the day for their first meeting finally arrives. Svend will come from his home in Copenhagen to Elsinore Hostel where there is an event that night. It is June 22, 1966.

Anne Sofie is nervous and cannot eat anything. How will he be in reality? Will they be able to have good conversations together, how does he look, how will he react when he sees her, and so on. The 17 year old girl walks restlessly around the dormitory, puts on her finest clothes, and tries to breath calmly. "Anso (an endearment), your father is here now" calls the teacher Tage Lau from the foyer. Her heart stops, now the big moment has come. She pinches herself and walks downstairs.

There stands her father, the engineer, with the teacher. He is not particularly tall, impeccably dressed in white dress shirt and suit, as he would for work when representing his company. He is handsome. And warm. And open. And loving. The first thing he says is, "How you look like your mother!" He knew her when she was around the same age as Anne Sofie is now. The excitement and her father's straightforwardness and kindness becomes too much for Anne Sofie who starts sobbing loudly in front of him, the teacher, and several of her curious friends. The teacher suggests father and daughter be alone for a while and they drive to a nearby forest in Svend's nice, new, red car to have some peace and talk quietly and calmly.

And how they talk. Svend cannot understand that Helene never got married and eagerly he asks about Anne Sofie's childhood, youth, and family and he also proudly tells her about his own family to whom he would like to introduce his newfound daughter.

His wife and the two children, however, have just gone to the family's summer house on Bornholm but he will write to his wife for permission to bring his big daughter there for the rest of the vacation.

That night Svend invites his daughter to a restaurant where they continue their conversation. He is sorry to hear that she grew up without a father figure, that there has not been a man in their home. He talks about adopting her but Anne Sofie knows that her mother would never agree to that. The restaurant also offers live music and when they play the song "Big Brown Eyes", Svend asks Anne Sofie to dance. To this day, the image of the newfound family happiness is engraved in her memory whenever she hears that song. Anne Sofie has found peace of mind and she is looking forward to the days to come when she will get to better know her family.

But before any vacation on Bornholm can be considered, Anne Sofie has to go with her classmates around Denmark and visit several attractions and cities. During these trips she speaks on the phone with her father many times and he is also able to visit her at many places, some in connection with him standing in for his colleagues in Jutland.

In Fredericia, Svend joins the Greenlandic youths once again and he invites Anne Sofie to visit his older brother Knud who lives there with his family. Happy and proudly Svend introduces Anne Sofie as his daughter but she experiences no hospitality there. Instead they are met coldly and with rejection and the visit is cut quite short. For Anne Sofie it is merely a preview of what she will later encounter, but nevertheless it warms her and makes her happy that her father, for her sake, defies his brother's rejection of her.

◎ Aarhus
June 26, 1966

Dear Ruth!

Welcome home from a presumably much needed vacation. Britta and the children went to Bornholm Tuesday morning the 21st. I followed them to Dragør from where they continued on through Sweden without me and they have arrived safely in Ypnasted. I have spoken with Britta on the phone and also received a couple of letters.

Anne Sofie called Monday night the 20th so it was fortunate that I was able to go and see her at Elsinore Hostel where they had school camp. I stayed and participated in the closing celebration.

Thursday the 23rd, Midsummer's Eve, they had arrived at Fredericia (on their Denmark tour, they are approximately 30 students), here Anne Sofie and I visited Knud and Jenny for a cup of evening coffee and then we went to the hostel and had Midsummer's Eve bonfire.

Today, Sunday the 26th, I ran into the group in Old Rye from where the trip went to Øm Abbey as well as Himmelbjerget and onwards to Aarhus where they are spending the night. Tonight we are all going to the theater in the Old Town where they are showing a play by Holberg.

Until July 15th I will be at the storage in Kolding phone number xxx-xxxx as our storage manager has gone on vacation in Italy for 3 weeks.

From the 27th of this month through approximately August 5th, Anne Sofie is staying with Doctor Ruth Mørch, Hagavej x, København, Søborg, phone number xxxxxx.

As of now, I expect to be in Copenhagen 7.16-7.26 and then I will leave for Bornholm. After August 5th to approximately September 14th, Anne Sofie is going to Vendsyssel and to school at the same time. Personally, I think she is a sweet and natural girl and, incidentally, looks a lot like her mother 20 years ago.

Well, that was what I had to tell, it has been lovely spending time with her these couple of times, so I look forward to seeing her a little more to get to know her even better.

The most loving greetings,
Svend
– it would please her to meet you. Svend.

The days go by and everyone returns to Zealand. The young people are housed at several different locations, Anne Sofie and her girlfriend Magga are living in Søborg with the Danish doctor Ruth Mørch whose children Anne Sofie had babysat earlier in Nuuk. One day Svend calls and asks if the girls want to see Copenhagen the following day. They will of course love to and they plan that he will pick them up in his car and show them the city.

The girls wait and wait but Svend does not show up in Søborg. At the end of the day the aunt from Fredericia calls and tells them that he is not coming because he has been in a car accident between Kolding and Fredericia and is hospitalized at a Jutland hospital. They will try to transfer him to Bispebjerg Hospital where his sister Ruth works as a nurse. The aunt does not mention how serious Svend's injuries are and Anne Sofie does not know what to believe. A few days later she receives an urgent telegram saying that she has to come to Bispebjerg Hospital as quickly as possible. Her father's condition is very critical and he keeps talking deliriously about Anne Sofie. When she meets her Aunt Ruth at the hospital, Ruth tells her that she believes the reason for the car crash could be that Svend was very depressed that day. He had received a letter from his wife Britta who did NOT want him to bring his newfound daughter with him to Bornholm with the rest of the family. That had made Svend lose his composure as he had promised Anne Sofie to bring her there and now he had to tell her that it was not possible after all.

Anne Sofie now meets his father's wife for the first time and she is seemingly accommodating and friendly towards her. They try to communicate with the seriously injured Svend but all they accomplish is that they can see him registering their presence. Britta promises while both Anne Sofie and Ruth are listening that she will take good care of her and make sure that she gets to know her half siblings. Svend is transferred again, this time to the municipal hospital where the doctors establish that his entire diaphragm is shattered and it is only a matter of hours how long he can be kept alive. Anne Sofie's world collapses entirely. It has only been three weeks since she met her father for the first time and now he is dying. The doctor in the white coat meets Anne Sofie, Britta, and Ruth in the hallway. They can tell by his facial expression that Svend has passed away. It is July 15th, the time is 4:30 PM.

Anne Sofie, Britta, and Ruth say farewell to Svend in the hospital room and the following days Anne Sofie is almost in shock. She does not remember much of what is going on, only the feeling of the complete unfairness. Why? She had finally found her missing father and he was everything she had dreamed he would be and she was going to get to know him and her family in Denmark. And then he just dies, three weeks after their first meeting. The young girl receives much consolation and care from her Aunt Ruth, grandmother, Uncle Bent and his English wife, and from Svend's own Aunt Grethe. They all accept her and understand her sorrow and frustration.

After a few days Aunt Ruth asks Anne Sofie to consider her father's funeral. Would she be very upset not to attend? Her Aunt explains that Britta is afraid of having a nervous breakdown during the funeral and that she is having difficulties having to explain to her children the existence of their sister with such short notice. Anne Sofie would like to show as much consideration as possible to her father's wife and agrees to stay away on the difficult day.

Instead she visits her Cousin Verner who is attending the machinist school in Hundested with some other Greenlanders. She is weighed down by sorrow but needs to be with other people and at night when the youths want to go out, Anne Sofie comes with them in order to not be alone. Her thoughts, however, are with her father's family – he was buried that same day – and she chooses to leave the party. As she walks through the woods to her cousin's house, she cries and screams and tells her father off for having left her so soon.

She does not see Britta anymore. Aunt Ruth makes several attempts to convince her sister-in-law to arrange a meeting between Anne Sofie and her siblings but every time the reply is that there is no way that will happen. It will have to wait until the children have turned 18 years of age, Britta believes. Aunt Ruth thinks that the real reason is that Britta is afraid of the reaction from her posh lawyer family who will hardly look favorably on the fact that her husband had a "bastard" daughter with a Greenlandic woman. Anne Sofie feels that particular reason as a very hard slap in the face.

In the other part of Svend's family – with his siblings, mother, and aunts – there is also unease and minor battles after his death. This part of the family are very faithful catholics and several of them have a very tough time accepting that Svend converted and became a protestant in connection with his marriage with Britta. That he is now dead is "God's punishment", thinks one of his aunts. On his deathbed, Svend once again turned towards Catholicism and spoke about forgiveness and about doing penance for the damage he had done to Anne Sofie by not being there during her childhood. This causes several controversies between his siblings as the following letter from his sister Ruth to his brother Knud shows.

February 20, 1967

Dear Knud –

From mother I have learned that you are amazed that I have not thanked you for your Christmas present. With the way our relationship had evolved, I thought it was rather inappropriate. I had expected a completely different present which I actually think you owe me after what happened after Svend's death – namely that you and I would talk things over.

At first, I thought you were acting strange because people often have intense reactions to great sorrow. But afterwards, one is normally able to see clearly again.

What I am aiming at is that you should know that it has caused me much pain that you as a Catholic in the conversation at my house after Svend's death have questioned Svend's sincerity in regards to his wish to see Father Poppe and receive help from the church. Do you think that if he had not wanted it that I in any way would force him into this? – He got the offer – and he accepted it willingly with all his mental faculty – and never had Svend been more in his right mind than in that moment.

With your negative attitude you allowed yourself to disapprove of the thing that we saw him finding much comfort and peace in.

Concurrently, I can inform you that Svend had already, before my trip to India, spoken positively in regards to reconciling with the church – on behalf of his children, too.

When someone you care for is on the edge and is being tormented by problems and worries – and in the end his mental aches were great – it is our duty to relieve them as much as we can.

His greatest problem was Anne Sofie. To him, the only solution was that his daughter be accepted. He kept asking for her because it was clear to him that he would not recover from the accident.

She did not make it before he lost consciousness. But following the psychiatrist's advice, she came to see him to brighten up his mind, if at all possible.

At that point she was very valuable to Britta. That was not the case before nor apparently after.

Your attitude in this whole matter is perhaps the most disappointing. At my house, you clearly conveyed a petty bourgeois and narrow minded opinion in the whole Anne Sofie matter. It had to be hushed up, concealed, and the girl should for any cost be kept away from her father's funeral.

Do you realize how wronged she has been?

After the shock and terrible time she unknowingly came to experience, you were as negative at this point as in any way possible and influenced Britta in a very unfortunate way, seeing that she had promised Svend to also take care of his eldest daughter (she heard her say it).

Anne Sofie has felt nothing from this promise and is undoubtedly finding her family down here highly peculiar.

What could have turned into something fruitful and constructive for Britta – to continue in the spirit of Svend, to make up the damage done to this child that he at any cost wished to make up – you have helped ruin. And I can assure you that it is the certain way to afflict her with some kind of neurosis if she does not realize this clearly.

No more about this. I had expected that you yourself would have felt a need to discuss these things. But upon receiving your last letter I understood that that was not the case – and that they are already being covered up.

To me, this is a serious business to cover up – and if you cannot see it yourself, I am afraid that we no longer speak the same language.

Thank you for notifying me of Inger's wedding.

Loving greetings,
Ruth

◎ August 14, 1967

Dear Britta,

It was sad that you ended the conversation so suddenly the other day because I don't think we were done talking about Anne Sofie.

You said that your children were not to know of their half-sister's existence until their 18th year – in order to not lose respect for their father. Now, there are many ways of explaining a matter, Britta. Don't forget that Svend and Helene Isaksen were engaged and that he sent his betrothed down to his parents for six months to get to know the Danish customs. That it did not end in marriage was not Svend's fault.

12 and 15 year old children today are much more advanced than parents normally think in regards to the deeper meaning of life. You can be certain, Britta, that your children will never be able to forget their father as the person he was to them – even if they were to hear the news about their oldest sister, and I am convinced that they will receive that piece of news with excitement when they get to know the fine girl.

You also said "when Svend hasn't told them himself during those six months..." that you are not going to either. What nerve you have to say it that way, Britta – you, who to the very end fought him tooth and nail to keep him from letting the children meet. He asked you to let Anne Sofie follow him to Bornholm and you know how fervently he wanted this. You spoke of brutality on the phone. Don't you think you can turn this expression on yourself in the given situation with Svend?

It is very unnatural for a widow not to continue where her husband left off. In this case, however, it was his last wish that was the matter – and the only thing that absorbed him.

Perhaps you have forgotten that you took Anne Sofie's arm by his sick bed and said "She is coming home with me". But perhaps that was an entirely hollow promise which carries no meaning to you after Svend passed away. Both Anne Sofie and I heard it.

I think it must be terrible for you to live in eternal fear of other people asking the children about their big sister's wellbeing – and it will most likely happen that way – since every normal person takes it for granted that the children know each other in our modern times. The only thing you achieve by stalling the children knowing each other is that they will lose their respect for their mother.

It is also peculiar that you not for a second think that Anne Sofie has feelings that you are hurting. She tells me that she has written to you several times without any reply. Did you have to go that far after having promised Svend to take care of her?

If I were you, I would consider this case one more time. Anne Sofie has 14 days left of her vacation and you and your children are welcome at my house where we can arrange a meeting. If you prefer not to come, I will be happy to do it on my own.

An entirely different matter which I regret to have to bring to your attention, but which I feel I have to for mother's sake, is that Svend owed mother a payment on your house mortgage. According to mother, it was due on April 1st this year. I assume that it is an oversight that you have not mentioned it to mother and wished a postponement of the payment. But with the way mother's finances are, she cannot disregard an amount of that size.

In regards to you keeping your children away from Svend's family, or parts of it, since Svend passed away, I will take the liberty to make a final remark: it is one thing if you do not yourself feel the need to see us, but you have no moral right to keep the children away from their aunt or Svend's siblings.

Ruth

In the time following Svend's death and funeral, Anne Sofie has to continue her program for her stay in Denmark with her schoolmates. They are being "stationed" different places in Denmark to get to know Danish families, everyday life, and school. Anne Sofie is placed in the North Jutland Tårs where she stays at a farm with a widow, a few of her adult children, and a lot of animals. She goes to school, makes a couple of girlfriends but does not remember much of the stay as the mourning of her father still absorbs her. On her 18th birthday she is invited to her grandmother's in Odense where Aunt Ruth also visits and is looking forward to spending time with the family.

Later, all the schoolmates meet again after their individual stays around the country. The reunion is a great joy and Anne Sofie feels the compassion and comfort from her friends when she tells them what has happened since they last met. She also writes to her mother in Nuuk and tells her everything about her experiences during the long stay in Denmark. But when she arrives home there is not much consolation or help from her. Though she is very sad to hear what has happened to Svend, she does not wish to speak with Anne Sofie about it.

Anne Sofie's life moves on, school continues, and she gets through the fall, partly through an intense correspondence with her grandmother and Aunt Ruth who both take their time to listen, read, and write with her. Anne Sofie desperately wants to get in contact with her brother and sister and get to know them but accepts Britta's decision to let Svend's two youngest children live in ignorance of their oldest sister, even if it hurts.

The following summer, in 1967, Anne Sofie is in Denmark on summer break. She works as a healthcare assistant at Bispebjerg Hospital for a month and lives with Aunt Ruth. Repeatedly they try to get in contact with Britta, they write and send gifts but without any luck. Anne Sofie is hurt and does not understand it but slowly, a defiance and a courage to fight against the injustice grows in her. She will no longer be treated that way and when she returns home, she decides to write to her brother Per. She does not expect him to receive the letter if she sends it to his private address and instead she puts the address of his school on the letter, the Catholic school in Nørregade.

◉ Nuuk
November 1, 1967

Dear Per,

You must find it strange to receive a letter from Greenland from a person you have never heard of nor seen with your eyes. I hope you will not be startled when I tell you who I actually am.

My name is Anne Sofie Isaksen, born August 28, 1948 in Qaqortoq, South Greenland. Daughter of a Greenlander named Helene Isaksen and my father is Svend Weber, that is, your father. I go to secondary school in Nuuk, I will graduate next summer. I was engaged in Denmark on August 19 at Aunt Ruth's.

So, I am your unknown sister whom your parents have been hiding since I was born. As you know, Svend W. was in Greenland as an engineer from 1945-51 and after this went to Greenland twice. While Svend was in Greenland, he was engaged to a Greenlander, Helene Isaksen and later, he sent her to Denmark so she could get to know Danish society. My mother lived with my grandmother and aunt at Ålykkehaven xx in Odense.

Per, the reason I am writing is that I would like to be in touch with you and Annette because I do not have siblings, I am a lonely child and my Mother is unmarried. I know all about you – I even have pictures of the two of you. I know your mother, I spent time with her while father was ill at Bispebjerg Hospital from where he was transferred to the Municipal Hospital and died July 15, 1966 at 4:18 PM. I was in Denmark at that time and in 1960 as well as this summer. I have seen all my family in Denmark except for Uncle Knud's daughter. They all know me but they hide it because they know that Britta does not want you to know that you have a sister in Greenland.

Last year and this summer I was on vacation in Denmark where I lived with Aunt Ruth and were in France together August 4-August 12. As you know, Aunt Ruth is now in Kinshasa in the Congo.

Per, Britta does not want you to know who I am, but please try to make her tell you about me and why she would rather avoid me when I am in Denmark this summer. If you are interested, I can send you a picture of me and I can tell you about my Greenlandic family in the next letter if you are even going to reply to my letter. I do hope that you will reply to it. My letter might seem very complicated and confusing in your eyes, that is because I cannot gather the sentences – but hope you understand the meaning of this letter. Say hi to Annette, my sister.

The most loving greetings,

From your sister Anne Sofie Isaksen, Box xxx, Nuuk, 3900 Greenland.

Answer me, Per, you will ease my life if you do. Do try and talk with your mother if you have the courage.

P. S. You may think I look like a real Eskimo, I look a lot like Svend and have blond hair and a light complexion. Most people think I am Danish.

◉ Nuuk
November 25, 1967

Dear Per,

Per, I hope you have received my letter which I sent to you a month ago. I sent the letter to your school because I know Britta will tear my letter apart if I send it to I. E. Ohlsensvej.

I hope you understood my letter, even if it is confusing. Per, do try to reply to my letter. I would very much like to hear from you and Annette. I would very much like to have contact with you as my real siblings.

Per, tell me how you felt when you received a letter from Greenland from an unknown person you had never seen or heard of. Did you tell Britta that you received a letter from your half-sister Anne Sofie? What would you like to be, Per? Are you going to upper secondary school after secondary school or what? Do you have any plans for the future? Per, if you reply to my letter, I will tell you more about me and my family.

Aunt Anna has now found her peace, it was good that she had a quiet and peaceful death. I shall never forget her, a wonderful and lovely person.

Yes, we now have Christmas spirit in the stores, it is so lovely and now we have had some snow. Yes, you should see how wonderful we have it up here.

Well Per, do me a favor and write a letter to your half-sister. Say hi to Annette and Britta.

The most loving greetings
From your devoted Anne Sofie

And then finally…

◉ Copenhagen
November 20, 1967

Dear Anne Sofie,

Many thanks for your letter. I just think it was a sneaky way you reached out to me but let's not fall out over that. Your way of thinking about my mother is wrong. It is something that happened outside the marriage so it is true, as my mother says, that what has happened before my time is none of my business if I am not interested in it. In other words, she does not want anything at all to do with this, she has 2 children already and that is enough for her.

You wrote that you would like to get in touch with Annette and me but you can only have connection with me, as Annette will not at all be able to understand any of this and she has enough to worry about as it is. You just have to promise me two things if you want to write to me, first: make no attempts to direct Annette's attention towards who you are and that you exist. Secondly: I will ask you not to get in touch with my mother either when you are here in the country or when you are in Greenland.

I spoke with my mother and she said that she could not forbid me from writing to you. I will very much like to write with you if you fulfill those two things and I hope you do. If possible, I would also like to have a picture of you and hear a little about your Greenlandic family. I have always been interested in Greenland and the Greenlanders, and I also intend to go there on vacation when I am older and can afford it. I was born June 8, 1952, my sister July 7, 1955. I collect stamps and have a good amount of Greenlandic ones but I would like to have more. I will ask you to write to my home, I spoke with mother about it. I live in Copenhagen.

Loving greetings, Per

◉ Nuuk
November 28, 1967

Dear Per!

Many thanks for your much appreciated letter which I received today. Thank you for the cute picture of you. It was nice of you to want to write with me. Per, what do you mean that it was a sneaky way to get in touch with you? Per, I cannot do anything else but write to you. This summer Aunt Ruth and I tried several times to contact you but fruitlessly since Britta doesn't want it and will not see me.

As you request, I shall contact only you – you bet I will and the two of us can always find each other. It was nice to hear that you are interested in Greenland. Yes, it is very wonderful up here, you will love it as father also did. Coming up here on vacation I think would be a great idea and I would like to be your tour guide, for I have sailed the entire coast from Prince Christian Sound to Upernavik – and been to most of the villages on the West Coast with mother who has sailed on the tuberculosis boat Misigssût along the entire West Coast up to Thule for 4 years, so she knows the entire West Coast as well her own pocket.

Now I shall tell you a little about my Greenlandic family. My grandfather had been manager of the trading posts in several villages in southern Greenland, died in 1949 of tuberculosis which was a common illness back then. My grandmother who is still alive is 60 years old, lives in Qaqortoq and her three siblings are still alive and in good health. She just returned home from Denmark, having been on vacation in Lyngby since early August with her youngest daughter's daughter who is 5 years old, and in 1964 she also went to Denmark on vacation for 14 days.

My grandmother has given birth to a total of 18 children including 2 twins, but only 9 of the children are alive now. The oldest of them is Johanne age 42, married to a boatyard manager in Holsteinborg and has 6 children. Next is my mother Helene age 40, works at the outpatient clinic in Queen Ingrid's Hospital as an interpreter and medical secretary. The third is Kristine, married to a telegrapher and has 7 children, she is 38 years old. Oluf who has sailed for many years on the big foreign ships from Denmark is now in Hundested as a fisherman, he is 37 years old, and then Adolf married to a Dane, lives in Lyngby, has two children and is a trained carpenter. He has been in Denmark since 1956. Olivie who is 27 years old, married to a carpenter, lives in Smidstrup by Hvalsø, has 4 children. She is a trained nanny, moved to Denmark when she was 16 and has never since been back to Greenland. Then Bibiane, married to a Greenlander who is managing the produce store in Qaqortoq, has 5 children and works at the dental clinic. Karl who is in Denmark now, studies medicine in Copenhagen and is 24 years old. Kasper is also in Denmark, he is a healthcare assistant at Vordingborg Hospital, he is 22 years old. Cicilie, the youngest of the pack, has been a flight attendant in Narsarsuaq for 5 years, flown from Narsarsuaq to Reykjavik and has now returned home to Qaqortoq and has a 5 year old daughter. You can see that 5 of the children live in Denmark and may do so for the rest of their lives. Then I have a cousin who is a machinist apprentice at Hundested Motor Factory, he is 19 years old like me and graduates in February. Another cousin who goes to Rungsted Gymnasium (High School) is 21 years old, he will also continue to study medicine.

Then there is me, Anne Sofie, born August 28, 1948, currently living in Nuuk, I am now in lower secondary school. I want to be a nurse like Aunt Ruth. First, I have to be a housemaid for 6 months starting in August, perhaps close to Odense because I would like to be close to grandmother, now that Aunt Ruth is away. I would like to be near her.

After that I am going to Fårevejle folk's school for health services on February 1st 1969. I have been accepted and if I make it through, I am going to Bispebjerg Hospital. I have received their application forms and talked with the matron. Everything else is as it should be but it all depends on my grades. This summer I worked at Bispebjerg Hospital from June 26 to July 23 in the medical department and that was an experience for me. From there we went to Løkken on vacation with Aunt Ruth and grandmother for a week where we stayed at the Danish Nurse Council's vacation home. After that we had 4 days of vacation in Denmark and went to France on August 4th on a 10 day vacation, we travelled with Amager Travels by train. We travelled through Germany and Belgium and made stops in the big cities and made a stop in Paris where we spent 4 hours and then left again for Bretagne to Dinard on the coast where we then stayed at a beach hotel. It has been an experience for me, it was lovely in France. I have also been to Iceland, Scotland, Norway, and Sweden, that was in 1960.

Per, you asked me when I am going to Denmark. I do not quite know yet. I think it will be in the month of August, I am going for 6 months – it is 100% that I am going. Per, I am engaged to a young man named Arne Hardenberg Heilmann, he is a Greenlander, and 21 years old. He is currently in Denmark. He does not live far away from you, he lives on Livjægergade xx, on Pension East. He is studying to become a civil engineer. He came to Denmark August 1st and is coming up here December 18 when he will be working for a year with the engineering company in this city. Per, if you would like to get in touch with him before he leaves, you are more than welcome to do so. He knows you, I have told him about you, his phone number is TR xxxxx. I can write to him if you respond to my letter whether you perhaps would like to meet with him, he is also visiting Aunt Grethe before he goes home, perhaps you can meet there.

Per, it is obviously up to you what you think about meeting him or not but I think you should do it because he is a very pleasant young man. He also has some slides from Greenland that you would enjoy seeing. Aunt Grethe and Bent have also seen them. He speaks fluent Danish, as they speak Danish to each other in their house, so he can also tell you a little about his family.

Per, what are your hobbies? I am mostly interested in skiing, cooking, sewing, and long hikes in nature. I am sending you two pictures of myself. I can tell you that now I have entirely short hair, I had it cut in France because of the heat.

Yes, it is quite lovely up here with snow and the long, dark days and Christmas spirit. Oh, it is wonderful. Per, now I bid you goodbye.

The most loving greetings from your big sister, Anne Sofie.

P.S. Aunt Ruth is doing pretty well in Kinshasa. She wrote that all plants are blooming in the most gorgeous colors, and that they are busy caring for the wounded mercenaries from the violence.

Christmas 1967

Dear Anne Sofie,

Many thanks for your letter and the beautiful pictures. You asked me in the letter what I meant with it being "a sneaky way you got in touch with me", by this I mean that you should have sent it to my address and not to the school because it proves that you are scared of mailing it to my address, that you knew my mother did not want you to get in touch with me.

In regards to your fiancé Arne Hardenberg: I would rather meet him later because what should we talk about? My hobbies are: radio, tape recorder, speakers, bike, moped, cars, swimming, biking, and stamps. You were, by the way, very lucky when you sent your first letter to me because when "sister" received it, there was a parent-teacher meeting the following night so "sister" might have given it to my mother and then I would most likely not have received it when she saw who it was from, so you were quite lucky there. Would you mind telling me a bit about Nuuk in the next letter? Whether it is a fishing town or an industrial town. How many people live there and where you live. Do you rent an apartment or do you live at the school?

In regards to my future, I plan to take the upper secondary school exams and then go to the apprentice school i Hvidovre and then on to technical college and finally become a technical engineer. My room looks like this (see color insert).

We are also getting into Christmas spirit here in Copenhagen. The store fronts are decorated and Østerbrogade, if you know where that is, is decorated with columns of pine and lights.

Loving greetings, Per

◉ (undated)

Dear Little Brother,

Thank you for your much appreciated letter – it was lovely hearing from you.

Per, I can tell you that Nuuk is an industrial city. There is a large fishing industry, there are approximately 6,000 people living there, and that is of course not a lot compared to those cities in Denmark, but it is the largest city.

From Nuuk to Maniitsoq is approximately 150 kilometers, a 6-8 hour sail from Nuuk. Do you know anyone there?

I live in a large health care facility that holds four nurses in total. It belongs to the health care administration and my mother only pays for lights and heat, I think. It is not even a part of the school, I moved away from the dorm because there was never any peace up there. There are approximately 200 people in the dorm & the students from the teacher's college.

It is a big school. I shall send you pictures from all parts of Nuuk, I shall buy some film and send it to Denmark for developing. Then they can send the pictures to you and I can pay the bill. I can do that after Christmas when I have settled down a bit. I also have a Christmas present for you, that I can send too, right after Christmas if you would want me to send you anything.

Per, I had seen your room before, or your apartment, back when Bent lived in your room for the month of July 1966 (so you have everything home with yourself).

As you wish, Per, yes you can meet my fiancé when he returns to Denmark again, then all three of us can meet.

Otherwise we are doing pretty well up here. I know Østerbro very well, I spent almost every day there the last days before I went home.

I hope that you are all doing well, too. Yes, now we are able to ski, it is wonderful, it is my favorite sport, it may be that I attend the skiing championship in slalom and downhill skiing in April. If they take too much of my spare time, I won't. This Sunday I am teaching some Danes how to ski. It will be exciting to see how much they can do.

It is a good position you are aiming for. I want to become a nurse. The application is all set, all I need is six months as a house maid, either in Zealand or Funen, close to grandmother.

Per, I wish you and your family a very merry Christmas and a happy New Year. May you be well in the new year.

The most loving greetings from your big sister
P.S. sending you stamps, next time a full pack.

◎ Copenhagen
December 20, 1967

Dear Sister,

Many thanks for your letter with the sweet Greenlander on it. I only just received your letter today, it is probably because of Christmas.

I knew a girl who travelled to Greenland, Maniitsoq, but that was a few years ago now, she was a Greenlander.

There is also a lot of snow here now but I have not yet had the time to go skiing. Today was the last school day of this year. Tomorrow, the 21st, we are meeting at 8:45-11:00 AM and the 22nd from 10-12 PM we are going to the movies to watch "The Living Desert".

We have Christmas break from the 23rd to January 4th, both days included. I will wish you and your family a very merry Christmas and a happy New Year.

Loving greetings, Per

The ice is broken between Svend Weber's two oldest children and slowly they get to know each other through the many letters. Anne Sofie still dreams of an education as a nurse like her beloved aunt, but it is difficult to find a job with a family that would give her experience and maturity prior to completing life as a student.

As can be read from her letters to Per, she is engaged to Arne Hardenberg Heilmann who is studying to become a civil engineer in Copenhagen. The engagement does not make the relationship with her mother much easier; Helene does not approve of Anne Sofie's choice, she believes Arne seems sickly and that Anne Sofie is too young to get engaged.

Christmas 1967

Dear Aunt Ruth,

Thank you for your letter which I received yesterday. Aunt, I was actually doing pretty well since I moved away from the dormitory – I can be entirely alone away from all the noise. But at night, even the smallest sound can make me stiff with cramps but it is better now and otherwise I spend the night in Doctor Joensen's house. But Arne is arriving this Tuesday, then he can at least stay with me until I go to bed. He is coming with Esther.

I have not heard from Mrs. Varming and Reverend Vick has not replied to my letter and Ellen M, Miss Bisbo, I do not know how they are doing, but I assume they are well. Aunt, I would have preferred to be in Funen, close to grandmother, but if you think I should stay with Chief Physician Moltke, I can do so. It was for grandmother's sake I wanted to be in Funen.

Aunt, you cannot believe how happy I have become. I wrote to Per in the beginning of November because I could not bear it any longer – I wrote the letter to the address of his school. I told him who I am and why I would like to be in touch with him. He answered my letter immediately and completely understood and accepted since he wrote, even if it is a in sneaky way that I reached out to him, we will not fall out over it. Was that not nice of him? He wrote that I must promise him two things if I want to write with him; to refrain from reaching out to Annette, she is too young still, and secondly to never get in touch with Britta when I am in Denmark or from Greenland – Britta said that herself. Therefore, I must honor his wishes if I want to keep in touch with him and you know how much I care about that. In the next letter I told him about my family and sent him two pictures upon his request. He is very excited about them and wrote that I must tell him more about Nuuk. Aunt, I actually wanted to send a Christmas card to Knud but I do not know his address.

I, or we, are not going to Qaqortoq as the last ship or connection was on the 12th and I could not leave Dr. Joensen because one of the doctors went home to attend his father's funeral so he was in a predicament too.

Otherwise we are doing alright up here, but such terrible things are happening around us. Now the king of Greece has fled to Rome, and now there is talk that the end of the world will take place on the 25th at one minute after midnight Danish time – we just read it in Politiken. But we take no notice of it, if it is happening then let it happen.

Yes, I will honor your wish and attend Christmas mass at midnight. Yes, I had spoken with him several times. I had considered dropping math and have a good grade in arithmetic. I also do not like the boys looking down on me because I am the only girl in class who takes math.

You will have a wonderful Christmas Eve. It must be lovely to experience how they celebrate Christmas down there in Congo.

I wish you all a merry Christmas and a happy New Year and wish we may all start off the new year well.

The most loving greetings
from Anne Sofie

◎ Nuuk
January 30, 1968

Dear Little Brother,

I am very sorry that I have not replied to your letter sooner. You must not think I have forgotten you, little brother, you are always in my thoughts.

We are doing pretty well up here and now we have had a lot of snow and it is still snowing. You bet it is wonderful. My fiancé and I ski every Saturday and Sunday and have considered partaking in the slalom and perhaps downhill skiing Greenlandic Championship in March. My fiancé is living with me and we have quite a nice time – my mother is living with her friend, a doctor, and they will probably get married over the summer when I return to Denmark.

We have had a nice Christmas and it is nice to have some vacation. How have you been over the holidays? And how are you doing? I have received a letter from Aunt Ruth and she wrote that she had purchased a car – apart from that she is doing rather well. Per, have you written to Aunt Ruth since she went to Congo? – if you are not in contact with her, I think you should write to her – she would really appreciate your letter. And if you are not in contact with grandmother either, then write to her, I think you are big enough to contact them. Of course, you decide yourself whether you will do it for my sake, I will not pressure you in any way.

Per, please answer my questions. I will also ask you one thing: has your relationship with your mother changed since I started writing to you – it may sound strange to you, but please answer!

Per, we must not lose faith when we encounter opposition, we must try to smooth it out and be strong. We have father as our role model, he is the father I always wished for, I have looked up to him. The short time I have known him, he had been loyal, happy, and he is the type who tries to smooth out the bumps in the family. We must also remember that father was Aunt Ruth's favorite brother and grandmothers favorite son. We must fight in life to get as good an education as possible.

Per, now I shall send you your gift before it becomes too late. I sent you some stamps, next time you shall have some coins.

Little brother, take care.

The most loving greetings
From your Big Sister and Arne

◎ Copenhagen
February 3, 1968

Dear Anne Sofie,

I am calling to your attention that it is your turn to write. Is something wrong? Do you not feel like writing anymore?

All the snow has melted here so I have not yet been able to ski this year but perhaps a new bunch will fall, I hope so. Have you had a nice Christmas? How is it up there after the American bomber crashed? Does it have any impact on people, do you hear about it every day?

Yesterday, Friday, we had a "Feast of the Light" at the school, or rather in the Catholic Church which is part of the school. It is an old Catholic tradition where, in old times on this day, people walked around the city at night to every home with blessed candles and had them lit and then they would go to church together.

Of course that is not possible to do in our day which is why we walked around inside the church in a long row and then each person put his candle in a candleholder on the alter. It sure looked good with all those lights.

Now you must be well until next time.

Loving greetings Per,

P.S. I forgot to thank you for the stamps you sent me. So I thank you now. THANK YOU.

◎ Copenhagen
February 9, 1968

Dear Anne Sofie,

Many thanks for your letter, it was lovely to hear that you want to write with me. I thought you did not feel like it anymore. We have had a wonderful Christmas. We visited Uncle Knud and Aunt Jenny as well as Inger.

At the moment I do not have any contact with Aunt Ruth and grandmother. Perhaps one should but I do not always feel like it or have time for it. In regards to my mother, nothing has changed, we talk straightforwardly about things and help each other the best we can.

Many thanks for the stamps, it is gradually improving my collection. I am pleased to hear you are doing well.

This Sunday 2/11, I am going for a long 60-80 kilometer ride with my friends. We have done it before and think it is lovely to move both arms and legs, especially after such a cold and long winter.

On Thursdays each week we attend church but yesterday we were in one of the neighboring churches. It was a big church and pretty on the inside. The priest told us about the church, the images inside it, the pulpit etc. It was really interesting. Now I must end my letter.

Loving greetings, your brother, Per

◉ Nuuk
February 13, 1968

Dear Per,

I hope you have received the previous letter that I sent you. I hope you understand that it is not because I did not feel like writing anymore but now you have had the explanation.

I do understand why you would like to know about the B-52 that crashed up by Thule. I can tell you that when we heard that it had crashed, we were of course surprised and afraid that it would spread radioactive rays all over Greenland. But fortunately, what has happened is a very small thing and it is not dangerous. We hear about in in the news almost every day, of course. From my point of view, I think that both the Danish and the Greenlandic politicians are only now waking up from a beauty sleep when the big bomber crashed. I guess it is always like that, that when accidents occur, you wake from the sleep.

Now it is quite peaceful up here. We have had snow storms the past 2 weeks so the entire city is almost covered in snow. But it always looks so cozy and makes one think back at one's childhood because back then there was much more snow.

Now we are getting closer to the 2nd term, we start the 19th. We are learning arithmetic, math, Danish grammar, English grammar, and Greenlandic, but I am let off math and Greenlandic so I will have some days off. Next time is examinations, then one will find out if they have been studious enough during the course of the year.

I had a letter from Aunt Ruth. She sends lots of greetings to you. Yes, it must have been lovely to partake in such a tradition like the Feast of Light.

I am sending you a little present and hope you will find pleasure in reading it.

The most loving greetings from your Big Sister

Through the letters, while sister and brother gradually get to know each other more and exchange both big and small news regarding their everyday lives and the world around them, Anne Sofie's new family acquaintance also takes a dramatic turn on a very practical level. In addition to the fight for being accepted as a person and as Svend's flesh and blood on the emotional and personal level, the young girl must also fight a different down-to-earth battle – namely to be acknowledged as Svend's daughter in a legal and inheritance sense. Britta will not accept that Anne Sofie should have any right to inheriting from her father and in the end, the authorities demand a blood sample to prove that the two are actually father and daughter. Both Anne Sofie and her mother Helene must be tested so the probability of Svend being Anne Sofie's father can be calculated. This demand for blood samples does not improve the rather strained relationship between Anne Sofie and her mother who is still very opposed to Svend's daughter's contact to her family in Denmark. However, Helene finally agrees to being tested.

⊚ Nuuk
February 28, 1968

Dear Aunt Ruth,

Thank you for your letters, which I have received – It took them quite a while to get up here and it has been bad weather here the past two weeks.

I am glad that you got my Christmas greeting after all, even if it was delayed. It is rather funny to hear that you had told your secretary a little about Greenland. It was rather awkward or not nice of Britta that she returned your Christmas greeting. Aunt, I do not think that Per and Annette have received your Christmas letter because he has not mentioned it. I wrote and asked him whether he had been in contact with you or grandmother because I think it would please you to personally hear from him. He replied that he did not always feel like writing but he wrote that perhaps he should. I wrote and explained to him the sneaky way I wrote to him. I am cautious in writing to him.

I sure hope that the polio is not so serious and that you are doing well with the research. You got your own little car. It must be nice to drive around in it and see the surrounding areas.

Aunt, I understand why you do not want me to be drunk. I am very sensitive to alcohol. If I only have 2 glasses of white wine I can feel it, it only takes a very small amount. I am not going to do it again, there is nothing to be afraid of.

Yes, thank you, Arne and I are doing well together. But aunt, I have so many worries at the moment that I cry very easily. I cannot tolerate anything. My mother is getting worse and I just moved away from the nursing dormitory. Arne moved back home, I live with a female doctor but she is leaving April 16th but on April 10th she is moving down to the TB boat. I do not know why I cannot move in with them when I have had my own room with them before. Aunt, I am completely shattered, I will never get to go to them. I am terrified of seeing my mother, I get startled when the phone rings, when there is a knock on the door, because I always think it is mother calling or knocking. I always lock the doors as soon as I get home so she cannot enter.

She cannot bear the sight of Arne. She compares him to a nanny because he spends all his time with me as if he were unemployed, that he is better off being close to his parents since he always looks so sickly. What will I do when he becomes disabled, because that is a risk? There are many men in the world, I can always just find another. I am too young to be engaged. She does not even want to visit me in my room. She does not like his parents, does not want me to visit them –it is as if I have no family at all. She cannot even greet my mother-in-law and she told me that she always wants to greet my mother but she just always turns away when she sees her. It is true, I have seen it for myself. Now my mother-in-law does not want to greet her on the street because she knows that she does not treat me well.When I told Arne what she had said about him always looking so sickly and that he is at risk of becoming disabled, he started crying because he got an arrow in his heart from those words. He cried for an hour and could not stop and we both cried together for over an hour. Mother has also given Arne weak nerves, he cannot take it either. She will wreck us soon but we care more for each other. At this point I am in a state where I suddenly start crying without knowing what I am crying over. In class it sometimes happens that my eyes well up and I cannot keep up at all. Aunt, what shall I do? I never visit mother until it is absolutely necessary. I do not dare see her, I hate her, cannot stand to be with her, because she does not want Arne and sees him as a disabled person, as a helpless individual.

School is not going too well. I have a 7 grade point average and too much pressure from my mother, so I cannot focus. She will wreck me soon. I thought about telling her that I cannot take it anymore, stop thinking about me, you will lose me it you do not want Arne. It is up to you. It is best to leave this place as quickly as possible when I am done – Arne said that too.

In the situation we are in I cannot make mother do anything for me. I will not contact her either, she cannot be trusted, we have experienced that, Arne and I.

They do not even have a clue where I will stay when Mette (the doctor) leaves on April 10th, and examinations are fast approaching. I do not think they want me. Arne's parents said that if I have no place to live, I can move in with them. They are so nice and kind, I tell you aunt, I always feel really at home when I visit them.

Well, aunt, I will end it here for now. Greetings to you from Arne.

The most loving greetings from
Anne Sofie

The blood samples show that Anne Sofie in all likelihood is Svend Weber's daughter and it is decided that she, for that reason, is also entitled to an inheritance. The money – just under 10,000 DKK – will not be paid to Anne Sofie until she turns 21 years of age. These things, however, are hard for Anne Sofie to keep track of since the authorities have appointed a guardian for her who is to safeguard her interests. She is more consumed by her relationship to her siblings.

◎ Copenhagen
February 20, 1968

Dear Anne Sofie,

Many thousand thank you's for the book—you bet I like it. By now I have quite a great deal of information about Greenland. Last Sunday the 18th, I wanted to go skiing because it had been snowing for a few days and there was a great deal here in the city and normally there isn't so I thought that there would be even more in the country. We left, but the longer away from the city we went, the less snow there was, so I did not get to go skiing that Sunday either, but I hope there will be another opportunity.

I should also pull myself together and write to Aunt Ruth. Do you know anything about when you are coming here this summer? Do you have a tape recorder, radio, or record player? I have all 3 things. You probably have not seen them because I think I got them after you saw our apartment.

Unfortunately, I have nothing more to tell this time.

Loving greetings, Per

◎ Nuuk
February 29, 1968

Dear Little Brother,

Many thanks for your 2 letters which I have received and apologies for not writing sooner. There has been so much to do lately, especially homework, that I have not had time to reply to your letters. I just moved to another apartment because mother moved to the sub-station as secretary to the chief physician.

The past two weeks we have had rather dreary weather, it changes a lot so we have not had a chance to ski. Yes it must be nice to be able to cycle so far away, we do not have the option for that up here – I myself have had bikes the past 7-8 years.

You asked me if I have a record player: yes I do, and I just bought myself a lovely new one. The old one I gave to my fiancé's little brother. I also just gave away a tape recorder with batteries, also to my fiancé's youngest brother. I also have a wireless radio which I will keep for now because I do not want a big one while I am still in school, it would be too much hassle to carry back and forth. It is actually much better buying it up here, they are so cheap, up to 25-30% cheaper because there are no taxes, everything is so cheap up here.

In regards to aunt and grandmother, it is of course up to you but I just think it would be wise of you to write. I understand that you do not always feel like writing letters, especially because you are a boy. Is that not right?

Per, I expect to arrive around August first next summer or in the middle of the month, it depends on when people would like me as a house maid.

I am happy to hear you are doing well with your mother, because I was afraid I had done something wrong between you.

Per, I just thought about what you had written, that it was a sneaky way to contact you. Per, all summer long aunt has waited for your mother to tell you about my existence because it was father's biggest wish before he died. Aunt had invited you to dinner so that we could meet in a decent fashion but your mother does not want to because I would be there. Did you understand that? I hope you understand and my letter does not bother you. Tell me if you think it is too harsh or wrong or if you do not want to hear about some things I write about.

Besides that, we are doing alright up here and hope the same for you. A greeting from my fiancé.

The most loving greetings from your Big Sister

◉ Copenhagen
March 21, 1968

Dear Anne Sofie,

Many thanks for your letter. It actually did not matter that you did not write until now because I am also very busy at the moment. I do not really agree with you that girls are more diligent than boys in regards to writing letters, it varies a lot.

In regards to my father and you I would have preferred it if he had told me himself. I think that would have been the best. But what is done is done and it is alright as it is now in regards to you.

Here we can feel the summer is coming, it is almost sunshine and blue skies every day. It is lovely. I am also busy in school, like you, but it will definitely be wonderful in the summer with warm weather etc. You bet I look forward to the summer break.

If possible, could you please send me a Greenlandic newspaper? I started the book you sent me and you bet it is good and exciting. Many thanks for the stamps.

Loving greetings, Per

◉ Nuuk
March 28, 1968

Dear Little Brother!

Many thanks for your letter which just came in the door – it is lovely to hear from you.

Perhaps you were right about girls and boys being equally diligent with letter writing but my feeling is that boys are lazier when it comes to writing letters. I also agree with you that it would have been best if father had told you about me but what is done is done and it cannot be any different.

I will gladly give you everything you ask for, just say the word and I will get it for you. I shall send you "Atuagagdliutit", that is the Greenland Post, and the Youth Magazine. It is in both Greenlandic and Danish so you can understand everything and then you can see what has happened the past two weeks. The Greenland Post is published every other week but there has been talk about changing it to every week. The contents are still lacking a little. The Youth Magazine is published every week.

Yes, it is always interesting reading about Greenlandic scholars' lives in Greenland, what they think about the Eskimoes and the many difficulties they have endured.

Per, what are your thoughts in regards to summer break, are you going to camp or out travelling? Oh right, perhaps you are going to Bornhol, to your house in Ypnasted?

Per, I should probably ask you already now about what you would like for your birthday?

Perhaps you might want something Greenlandic so I can have time to get it for you.

Arne sends all his regards.

The most loving greetings from your Big Sister

P.S. The newspapers may come a few days later. It is wonderful weather outside so I am going skiing. We are currently practicing for the Greenlandic Giant Slalom Championship.

◎ Copenhagen
April 17, 1968

Dear Anne Sofie,

Many thanks for the newspapers. Yes, it is fun to read them.

We just got back from Easter break, we went to Bornholm. It was wonderful weather with sunshine and we also had warm weather. My summer vacation is not really planned yet but I can tell you what I have been thinking: from July 1st – July 15th I am probably going to North Zealand, Asserbo, which is where the school has a place they use for summer camps, weekends and camps during the school year. Around July 9th or 10th I am probably going to Boy Scout camp so that will affect events. The last 14 days of the break we are going to Bornholm. But perhaps I am going to Jutland, I shall wait and see whether I will have time for it all. There is actually nothing set in stone. I would like some kind of Greenlandic thing for my birthday if you wish to give me something.

When are you competing in the Greenlandic Slalom Championships? It is so crazy because I have a moped but I am not allowed to ride it for another 2 months. Do you have a moped? Or are you not able to ride mopeds up there? In 14 days we have our written examinations and the oral. That is not much time so I will be busy. When are your examinations? What did you do for Easter?

I will end for now.

The most loving greetings from Per. Say hi to Arne.

P.S. You should take into account that there are many who have a sister or brother that they do not know exists or never will get to know, but I am happy to have been told that you exist.

Nuuk
April 29, 1968

Dear Little Brother,

Many thanks for your letter, I am happy to hear from you again. It sounds good that you have read the different newspapers.

It must be wonderful to go sailing during the breaks. We do not have the opportunity to travel up here as the travelling options are very poor and expensive. I look forward to coming to Denmark where I can travel. I do not have a moped. I was supposed to get one but I did not want to anyway because it is only boys that have them. I plan to buy a bicycle at home. I can see that you will have a pretty busy summer break but we can meet at some time if that works for you.

I do not know yet where I will be for the six months as a house maid but my aunt's girlfriend is finding me a spot. I had written to her so I am very excited to see what she has come up with. I expect to be around Birkerød and Hillerød, that is what we agreed with her – then I am close by when Aunt Ruth is expected back in August for vacation. Do you even know that she turns 50 on May 11th? She would be very happy if you sent her a little birthday greeting.

Arne and I were not part of the Greenland Championship because our organization G.S.S had entered too late. They were supposed to enter by March 1st and only signed up April 4th. It is so difficult keeping up with what happens at the dormitory when you have moved into the city. They were very sad because we were not in it, another organization also told G.S.S. off because we were not in and because I had chances of winning the women's competition. I have been thinking that I should start doing cross country in Denmark or perhaps continue doing slalom, then Arne and I will register in a skiing club.

I too am very happy to have established a connection with you. I have always thought of you and your sister because I was told when I was a child that I had 2 siblings. In 1966 especially it was very nerve-racking because I wanted to see you, but because I wanted to spare your mother, I stayed away. Even though I knew where you were living and in which school you were, I did not go. I cried at Aunt Ruth's place and asked if I could see you even from a distance. Finally, only at the end of 1967, I was no longer able to stay away even though Britta had said that you would not be told until you were 18 years old.

Our written examination starts May 2nd and the oral examination comes right after Easter. I will be busy revising everything we have gone over throughout the year. I hope I do well. I shall try and find something for your birthday.

Yes there are quite a few driving mopeds in Greenland and in Nuuk. In Nuuk there is a lot of traffic – here are close to 500-600 cars in this city of 6,000.

I did not do anything during the Easter break. We went skiing and watched the Greenland Championship. It was really fun – it is 5-6 kilometers north and it takes an hour by ski but it has been lovely weather. At the moment it is snowing and it has been for the past week. That is annoying–we thought spring had arrived.

I will end for now. Arne says hi again.

The most loving greetings
From Big Sister

◉ Nuuk
May 19, 1968

Dear Little Brother!

Many thanks for your letter. I am happy to hear that you have written to Aunt Ruth. She will be very happy. Aunt Grethe also has her birthday tomorrow so I have sent her a card. I am certain you will go over there and visit her.

Now the end of the school year is approaching. We still do not know when we have our last day of school, but expect it to be around June 10th. For oral examinations we have Danish, history, English, math, Greenlandic, and French, however, I am not taking math or

Greenlandic so I am taking French with another girl, and we are only two, you see. I am very satisfied with the subjects.

Arne and I expect to be in Denmark at the end of the month of July because I expect to begin work on August 1st. June 28th I am going down to Qaqortoq because I am longing to see my birth city since I have not been there for 3 years. I am also very interested in seeing how big a change has happened down there.

There is a skiing club in Denmark, Arne said, because his friend Sten Balle is a member of Jutlandic Skiing Club. They also go to Norway or Sweden and ski but they also ski a lot in Denmark, even though snow is scarce.

It is not too bad with the examinations, and the material from lower secondary school is mostly just repetition with expanded material from the previous two years. If you just keep up in classes and read your homework, there is actually no problem with it. They are the exact same assignments we get back in Denmark. I expect that they are stricter at home. Up here they demand quite a lot of us but it can be rather difficult at times because we need to be bilingual, so additionally we need to learn English, German, French, and Latin.

At the moment we have the most wonderful spring weather. All of last week we had wonderful days with sunshine. Yes, now the snow has almost melted. Every morning I rise early to enjoy the fresh morning air. You see, I too live right by the water so I always enjoy the view. Every morning I walk 3 kilometers to school and it is lovely to get exercise daily.

I also wish you do well and good luck.

The most loving greetings
From Big Sister

◎ Nuuk
June 20, 1968

Dear Little Brother!

I hope you have received the present Arne and I sent you for your birthday. We hope you have had a lovely birthday.

I graduated lower secondary school on June14 as the first of 44 because the others are taking Greenlandic first and the last ones were done yesterday. It is weird not to have any homework, for now at least. The day I graduated, I was very relieved, it is as if some sort of heavy burden is removed from me. I shall miss the school a lot.

Today at 3 PM we receive our transcripts and tonight we are having dinner with the guests in the great dining hall at the dormitory. The oral examination went fairly well; 8 in Danish, 8 in English, 7 in French which took place on June 8. It was the translation that went wrong, and 9 in history, where I got lucky and drew the examination question I wanted – Germany after WWII and the UN and its sub-organizations. My written was bad, 7 in Danish essay and I think 7 in arithmetic, but on the other hand, I do not know what I got for English translation. It is probably bad because I do not know English, especially grammar. Besides that, Arne and I hope that you did well on your exams.

I have now started working at Queen Ingrid's Hospital. For now, I am working with my mother for the chief physician on the tuberculosis station, she is his secretary, you see. Next Monday I am transferring to the out-patient clinic where I will be working as an interpreter for 14 days and perhaps after that as an interpreter in the medical department. I am excited about it.

Two weeks ago I received a note from the matron at Bispebjerg advising me not to enroll at Bispebjerg's preschool until September

1, 1969, as they will no longer have courses for those who have attended nursing colleges. Thus, I expect to start as a house maid after Christmas, I just need to hear from Aunt Ruth what her thoughts are. I will probably stay here for Christmas but I might be going home on vacation with my fiancée. Because we have talked about that, we have already booked tickets.

My parents-in-law are all in Denmark. Arne's mother is going today with her son who is in a wheelchair, is going to Holbæk to the hospital for physically disabled. I will be housekeeping for them. There will be plenty to do because their house is being painted and wallpapered. Besides that, we are doing pretty well up here.

It has been lovely weather the past two weeks, sunshine, no wind. It is gorgeous, the ocean is smooth as a mirror when you wake up in the morning, for we live right on the water.

Besides that, be well and happy exams.

The most loving greetings from
Anne Sofie and Arne

◉ Nuuk
July 22, 1968

Dear Per!

Many thanks for the letter which I received today. I was starting to get nervous that you had not received our gift. Yes, it has been quite a while since you have written. I thought you had not received my last letter.

It is annoying not having any homework, I am getting tired of not having anything to do. For 3 weeks I have worked at the out-patient clinic as interpreter and now I am not doing anything and live with my in-laws helping them with this and that. Next Friday Arne and I are going on vacation to Qaqortoq and will return August 16th. So for now, my journey has been postponed one year, so I will be home when you have graduated. I hope you will not be disappointed, I am very keen on meeting you but unfortunately it will not be until next year that we meet.

It will be difficult getting to Qaqortoq because of the "storis" (east Greenland pack ice), everything is closed off all the way up to Paamiut. They say that there has never been so much ice since 1941, and that two coast ships cannot get down there. We will probably end up taking the helicopter down there.

From August 19th I will be a house maid for six months for a Danish family with three children. Besides that, we are doing alright up here. We have had some wonderful days with sun and warm temperatures up to 16-17 degrees celsius. We have not had rain until the last few days.

Per, did Annette turn 12 or 13 on July 7th? Yes, Aunt Ruth will soon return home to Denmark, around August 1st, if she can get a ticket. I am sorry I cannot greet her little brother. Aunt will be very happy to meet you but it is up to you whether you feel like meeting her. No one can forbid you to greet her! Little brother, I think you should be in my place when she returns home from vacation since I cannot be present. Do you understand that, Per?

I will hope you get some wonderful sunny days in Weber's house.

Be very well.

The most loving greetings from Big Sister and Arne.

The postponement of Anne Sofie's stay and education in Denmark is, however, not only based on the advice from Bispebjerg's matron and the lack of a house to be a maid in, as she tells her brother. For when she graduates in 1968, she is already aware that she is pregnant. So while the training as a nurse is put on standby, Anne Sofie chooses to become a house maid for six months with a Danish family in Nuuk. In spite of morning sickness she does her job and spends her time off preparing for her and Arne's own family life by knitting baby clothes, sewing cross-stitches, mending clothes and so on. The Danish family also introduces her to another food culture which she happily combines with her traditional knowledge. The patriarch's favorite dish is lemon soup and garlic is introduced in enormous amounts as Anne Sofie needs to learn that a clove of garlic is not the same as an entire head. She is also puzzled by the fact that she can prepare a single chicken and still have sufficient amounts of food for three adults and three children – a meat loving Greenlandic family would have never stood for that.

Even though the pregnancy was not planned, both Anne Sofie and Arne are happy with the circumstances. It does not matter to Anne Sofie that her education plans are postponed, for it is just a postponement and not her giving up her ambitions. Arne's parents receive the news about the family expansion very positively while the excitement is barely traceable for Helene who is not exactly happy with the prospect of becoming a grandmother. She definitely thinks that Anne Sofie should prioritize education first.

◎ Nuuk
September 1, 1968

Dear Aunt Ruth,

Many thanks for your letter from July 20. I am very sorry I have not replied sooner. You see, I have had so much to do and we have been on a 3 week vacation in Qaqortoq from July 26th to August 16th. There has been so much pack ice that we were cut off from the outside world, save for the helicopter. Now I shall tell you what I have to say and I know that you will worry about it all. As you know, I tell you everything.

As you know, we are staying up here for one more year because Arne has a one year contract. Therefore I have accepted an offer given to me. I started as a house maid with a Danish family on August 19th for six months. The man is a journalist in the Radio House, they have 3 children from 6 to 2, two girls and the youngest is a boy. They are very nice. The wife has a job in the afternoon, she always helps me with the morning cleaning, then I have the children the rest of the day. The oldest goes to kindergarten in the afternoon. I cook for the family, off every other weekend and a free period once a week. Then I am paid 400 DKK plus food and accommodation. It is pretty good. Arne lives with his parents. I also lived there for 2 months, but when school starts I can no longer live with them. You see, we have not yet found an apartment or room, it is very difficult here – 2 years waitlisted. We just received an offer though and hope it is not so expensive. Aunt, I have not seen my mother for 2 months, even though we live in the same city. I am in the city every day twice a day, and never see her. I moved away from her and cannot stand it anymore. She hates Arne and his parents but my in-laws wanted to invite them over for dinner several times. I usually say that she will not come, might as well not invite her. I still have my things in their place which I need to get this week, very interesting. She is also acting very strange towards her sister's family so they think she has gone crazy.

I had a lovely birthday. Arne gave me an oak wood coffee table and a wicker stool and a very cute lamp. From the in-laws a hand mirror and a vase of the same type as the lamp from Arne so that was very coincidental, and from the people I work for a candle stick with candle and a wooden bowl in the same color as my new coffee table. Then we also bought a pullout couch – we are slowly collecting.

I have written to Fårevejle and Bispebjerg and am waiting to hear back.

Aunt Ruth became great grandmother August 10 and it will not be long before she will become great grandmother for the second time. If it goes well and if nothing happens to me, I am due in the middle of February. We know that it is still too early but that does not mean the child is unwanted, we look forward to the day we have the child. I am thinking a lot about whether to train to become a nurse or for something else. It is something that should be pondered very carefully.

We are doing well with money up here. We put money in the bank and then we had a vacation in Qaqortoq and that was 3,000 kroner but we still have money to spare.

Aunt Ruth, we have also had some hassle with the inheritance from father. The case was brought up here in July because Britta was unwilling to give me the money but in the end she changed her mind. Mother and I were down at the police station to talk with a police officer who had received the case. Britta wanted us to take a blood sample, mother and me, because she wanted to make sure that I was his daughter. She was uncertain because she had only heard that Svend had a daughter and nothing else. Mother was of course outraged that we had to give a blood sample but in the end we convinced her because Britta demanded it. Now I have met Guldborg Chemnitz who is dealing with that and she has been to Denmark and has, among other things, talked to Britta and she said she would talk to me about it when she has time because she is very busy at the moment, translating in the Landsrådet (Greenlandic political organization) and has travelled with the royal couple in Greenland as translator. She said that Britta is very stubborn because she does not want to give me the inheritance. It probably will not be too long before I am talking with her.

Aunt, I cannot understand why she does not want me to contact her in any way and threatened that if I do, I will never hear from Per. I still cannot understand it.

I do not hope this letter disappoints you in any way. We are doing pretty well up here and Arne likewise. We send you the most loving greetings.

Anne-S. and Arne

Anne Sofie and Arne are looking forward to becoming new parents and would also like to get married as quickly as possible, especially after the family in Denmark receives the news and, with their Catholic faith, press on for a wedding before the child is born. But it is easier said than done. Before that, the couple wants joint accommodations and to establish their first home and they do not have enough money to cover both wedding and apartment. The wedding will have to wait a few months.

◎ Nuuk
September 10, 1968

Dear Per,

Thank you for your letter from August 26, it was nice hearing from you again. Well, how is it being in your 3rd year of secondary school, is there a lot do?

Per, you have made me one year older, I only turned 20. Yes, it is sad that I postponed my journey to Denmark for a year, I would have loved to start right away. One has to be mindful of one's fiancee.

I started as a house maid on August 19th for 6 months in the house of a journalist from the Radio House, they have 3 children, I get paid 400 DKK in addition to food and accommodation. I am very happy to be with them, they are ever so pleasant. As you know, I was not supposed to be a house maid until February but because we could not find an apartment or room, I accepted the offer. When I stop, I shall find a job in the city.

In regards to Ruth, I have not been told when she is coming to Denmark or if she is coming home on vacation at all. I doubt it. You see, it is so long since I have written to her – but now I shall do it – so she probably cannot understand why I have become so lazy with the correspondence.

I know Ole Dam and his wife very well. Ole Dam was my biology teacher for 2 years and his wife was my German teacher, they are very pleasant both of them. You can expect them to know me quite well, please send them my regards.

We have also had a nice vacation in Qaqortoq. The summer has been so lovely this year, it is wonderful. Now it is already getting cold, the other day we had sleet.

I will stop for now.

The most loving greetings
From Anne Sofie

◉ (undated)

Dear Per,

Did you receive my letter which I sent to you at the end of September? Why do you not write? I have become so anxious that you do not like writing with your big sister anymore. Since you are my little brother there is no way I will lose you.

I also received a letter from Ruth, she had been on vacation in Copenhagen. She was disappointed to not see you as she had otherwise expected.

Per, do not get offended when I say what I have in mind. I have a feeling Britta is on your back so that our connection will be broken off. Since father passed away she has worked hard to prove that I am not Svend's daughter so that I will not get any of the inheritance. Now the results have shown that it is undeniable that I am Svend's daughter. I also do not understand why she does not want me to have contact, it is probably because she has a bad conscience towards me. She is also acting strange, after having been so nice when father was in the hospital. Enough about that, I actually do not care about her.

I hope you understand me, it is embarrassing to me too as I do not wish in any way to be unfriendly with Britta.

I hope you are well and take good care of your homework so you can do well in your examinations.

I (we) are doing well up here. I can tell you that you will be an uncle in 3 months – you see I am expecting a child around the 22nd of February, it is a little too soon but one could be unlucky and forget a birth-control pill. We expect to get married in mid-December, it is not settled yet as we do not know whether we can rent a house. We expect to be able to borrow it, and should know one of these days.

Otherwise we expect to get married at the same time as we are having the christening. It will be lovely if we could borrow a place until we get our own apartment in May. Aunt Ruth, and Aunt Grethe encouraged us to get married as soon as possible so I wrote to them that we cannot afford to have a wedding.

It is my family (mother) who is paying for it but since we do not get along and do not see each other even though we live in the same city, I cannot count on her. I do not even think she would attend our wedding seeing she is much opposed to Arne and his family. At the moment Arne's father is in Copenhagen attending meetings. We will probably get married when he returns in December.

Apart from that, I hope you respond to my letter and tell me what you think it right. I will end for now.

The most loving greetings from
Anne Sofie and Arne

◉ Nuuk
October 28, 1968

Dear Aunt Ruth,

Thank you for your letter from October 20, which I received October 26, it is a shame that it takes so long to get the letters sent up here. You see, I was down at the post office and they put the stamps on themselves.

I received a letter from Aunt Grethe and grandmother a week ago and they told me that you have all been to Yugoslavia and it has been so lovely. Then grandmother got to travel a little around abroad, she must have been excited about that. It is quite a short time you were home, 8 days?

It was too bad you did not see anything of Per. He had promised to stay in touch with Aunt Grethe so he could have a fairly good idea of when you are home. I have not heard from him for a long time either so I wrote a letter in September but have not received a reply. I have a feeling that Britta is on his back, and I even have a great deal of questions that I would like to have clarified but I feel bad for him that I am always bothering him.

Yes, we too think it is much too soon, but it happens that one simply forgets to take one birth-control pill. Grandmother and Aunt Grethe also wrote that we should get married as soon as possible, we would like to do that but we cannot afford to get married at the moment, when we take into consideration Arne's and my family who would be going not to mention the clothes themselves. We still have not found a place to live, I have been allowed to stay here as long as we do not have anywhere to live, they are happy to help. They said that we should just let them know if there is anything we need. Arne just turned 22 on July 15th.Yes, I have had my appointment with the midwife, there is nothing wrong. She expects me to deliver February 22nd so there is nothing to worry about, I am doing well.

A week ago I got a response from Bispebjerg that I am able to get in January 1970 if I have passed folk high school exams and my health condition is satisfactory. I would like to have the nursing training if I can manage it but the only thing is that when I am to start in August 1969, the child will be only 4½ months old. It will be tough taking care of both the child and homework at the same time. I still haven't figured out what to do instead, could you please make a suggestion?

I have some letters here that you can read and see if they can be useful. It is three of father's letters, the third is from 1974 which he wrote to mother but unfortunately I cannot find the rest of it. I cannot talk to mother about whether she had seen father after her stay in Denmark since she does not think that it matters that I get that money from the inheritance, seeing she is much against it. I know, and she has told me herself, that she had been with father after she came home from Denmark and after she became pregnant and father knew she was pregnant with his child. I also asked my aunt about it, she said it is correct what mother had said.

Yes, we are saving money but we have started collecting oak furniture. I got an oak coffee table for my birthday from Arne and a very nice lamp and a wicker stool, we have also bought a sleeper for me and in early October an oak radio by Beomaster and two matching big speakers so we need a record player but we will wait for Christmas when that can be our present.You see, I have one that works pretty well. For I furnished my own room since they did not have any of those things.We also do not purchase anything with installments, I do not like it.

I do not think I have any more to tell, I hope you will understand us because you are the only one I can really trust. I certainly cannot count on mother, she changes opinions every moment. We hope you are well.

The most loving greetings
from Anne Sofie and Arne

P.S. From Arne's father Henning Holm we received two little baby shirts, they are very cute. They also just had a daughter on August 15th. His wife wrote that he is very proud of becoming a grandfather.

As is evident from the letters, it is a long and rough process for Anne Sofie to be accepted as Svend Weber's daughter – by both family and authorities. However, she receives loyal and stubborn support from her aunt who independently continues the fight by, among other things, contacting a law firm.

◎ November 29, 1968

Dear Mr. Kahlke,

Thank you for looking into the options for helping Anne Sofie with her inheritance case. I shall try to tell the history as objectively as possible:

My brother, Svend Weber, died on July 15, 1966 after a car crash and left a wife and 3 children of which the oldest daughter, Anne Sofie Isaksen, was born 8.28.1948 out of wedlock. She is the daughter of Helene Isaksen, Nuuk. My brother was engaged to Helene Isaksen and intended to marry her and for that reason he sent her to Odense in 1947 to live with my parents to learn Danish housekeeping. He himself was at the time an engineer on the meteorology station at Prince Christian Sound in Greenland. When Helene returned home again, I know she spent some time up at Prince Christian Sound. I myself was abroad in 1948 but upon my return I was told by my parents that Anne Sofie had been born – but that Svend did not want to marry her mother because she had been unfaithful to him. Back then he paid a one time payment – ridiculously small – of 400DKK, I think. In the years that passed, until 1966, I had never mentioned the subject to my brother because he did not mention anything himself – and because I thought it was his personal matter which was none of my business. But I know that he has seen his daughter since her birth.

In the fall of 1965, Anne Sofie got in touch with my mother whose address she had obtained from Helene Isaksen and requested her father's address. She was going on a school vacation in Denmark and after so many years, she wanted to get to know her family. I spoke with my brother about the whole thing – and he asked me to initiate the correspondence with Anne Sofie. He was very touched by the situation and would do anything to help his daughter. They wrote to each other and she came for her vacation, they met and he was delighted with her. His problem was then predominantly how he could make his wife accept her – and arrange a meeting between Anne Sofie and his other children, Per – then 14 years old – and Annette, then 12 years old. He wrote to my sister-in-law who was on vacation on Bornholm asking her if he could bring Anne Sofie there. This she most strongly opposed – it was downright excluded. The day he was in the car crash he had just received his wife's letter and he told me in the hospital that he could not understand how it could happen but that he had been mentally unbalanced. He was on his way to Copenhagen to meet Anne Sofie that night. He suffered many injuries and during his short stay he was very preoccupied with what would happen with Anne Sofie, then I called her to the hospital. When he later suffered an unexplained psychosis, the psychiatrist asked his wife to allow Anne Sofie to be present – and she agreed. She went so far as to promise my brother, while we were both listening, that Anne Sofie should go home with her. This promise she never delivered as she has not been willing to see her since his death.

Anne Sofie stayed with me that summer and came back the following summer when she worked at Bispebjerg Hospital as a nursing assistant and accompanied me on vacation in Bretagne. She hoped to get in touch with her siblings but all contact was broken off – and a very tense and almost hostile relationship emerged between me and my sister-in-law because I let her know that she should have acted differently in this matter. Anne Sofie went back to secondary school in 1967 to take her examinations which she passed this summer. She is now a house maid in Nuuk until next year where she was supposed to begin nursing training in Denmark – whether she will succeed I do not know because she got engaged during her stay in Denmark and is expecting a child in a few months.

What I worry about is that my sister-in-law is doing everything in her power for Anne Sofie not to be acknowledged as Svend's daughter because of the inheritance. I know that probate court cases can drag on but in my understanding it is now only Anne Sofie who is a hindrance for the estate to be assessed. I know that people are allowed to make statements in the probate court and if this information which I have can help her case it would please me much more as I feel this child has been wronged throughout the whole process.

When I drew up my will with you, you were so kind to investigate who her guardian was and I seem to recall that you said that my brother had been listed as legal guardian in the past. I therefore asked you whether it would be an advantage if I applied to become her guardian but you said that it did not matter much because she was living in Greenland.

Who her guardian is now I do not know but she writes that a translator for the Landsrådet (government), Guldborg Chemnitz (probably also the health visitor), has been in Copenhagen to speak with my sister-in-law Britta Weber, J. E. Ohlsensgade xx. In June this year they have prompted a blood sample to be taken from both Helene Isaksen and Anne Sofie by a police officer in Nuuk. Her mother is not at all interested in Anne Sofie maintaining her rights – in general, Anne Sofie does not have a good relationship with her mother who never understood her. The mother has remained unmarried and has been employed as an interpreter on Missigsut for a number of years. The mother will not get in touch with me, the letters I have written she has not responded to, so it is very difficult for me to penetrate all of this.

When Anne Sofie returned home from her last visit to Denmark, she got in touch with her brother Per and the two are now corresponding but she is not allowed to seek out his sister and the boy is not allowed to mention Anne Sofie's name to Britta, because she would forbid him to write. She is probably convinced that I have made her write to Per, that is not the case, however. But I think it is quite in order.

Attached is a letter from my brother to Anne Sofie's mother from 1947 which she has found herself. Also, letters from my brother to Anne Sofie written shortly before his death.

I know that her baptismal record says daughter of Helene Isaksen, unmarried girl. The name of the father is not mentioned.

Should there be anything else I can help with, I am more than willing to.

The kindest regards and thank you,
Ruth Weber

◉ December 29, 1968

Dear Miss Weber!

I now return to your letter from the 1st of this month regarding your deceased brother's estate. I have performed different investigations and I have been informed that the administration of the estate has been finalized and that the estate has been tried by one of the probate court's regular assistants, lawyer Svend Christensen. Your sister-in-law has been represented by attorney Holten Christensten. The latter has reported to me that his client sure enough has requested a blood type investigation et al.

These investigations, however, have shown that there is no doubt of the possibility of your brother being the father of Anne Sofie Isaksen and it has therefore been decided to waive the continuation of the case, thus allocating normal inheritance of the estate to Anne Sofie Isaksen.

Her guardian during the assessment of the estate has been, as your letter mentioned, Guldborg Chemnitz and there can be no doubt that the inheritance has been deposited to the Public Guardian and, thus, cannot be disbursed until Anne Sofie Isaksen has turned 21 years of age. I have hitherto not been able to be informed of the size of the amount.

I hope this information is sufficient, otherwise you will probably be able to learn more from the assigned guardian. I return the letters attached to your letter.

Kind regards,
Kahlke

ede det straks, som du ønskede det. Jeg blev nu
de brev, det er før anden gang jeg fik et så hårdt
det vil jo komme en dag, og nu er det jo s
ro altid af sine egne fejl.
skrev, at jeg sørgede dig den sidste dag – jeg vil
en måde faster. Jeg den morgen fordi jeg v
der var flere ting vi skal ordne inden jeg r
tale dig Ruth, den sidste uge jeg var hos dig
æret inde på et bur, jeg følte på dig og når du
l ondgå at jeg går over til Arne. Du var så
skal blive gravid, eller at der sker overhovedet
emlig føle det, når du taler til mig. Jeg skal
15 år og er 19 år – jeg ved, hvad jeg gør.
jeg tænker ikke kun på mig selv, det gør
u har fået den fornemmelse af mig. Ruth, du
fordi jeg havde helt glemt, at jeg skylder dig
mærkeligt, at du slet ikke havde husket m
havde penge, og du kunne have fået det m
l nok få det penge tilbage, jeg vil ellers ger
h; men jeg ved jo ikke hvad jeg skal gøre ve
meget jeg skylder dig – så er jeg fri for d
mere. Hvis du også føler dig narret for
rettere sagt, at den tid jeg havde boet hos
penge som du havde brugt til mig – du
bage, hvis du ønsker det. Hvis du, i det hele tag
f mig, kan du rolig afbryde forbindelsen me
ønsker jeg det ikke, da jeg ikke vil miste dig

Anne-Sofie, Spring 1967

Svend Weber in last known picture.

Anne-Sofie's parents

Above, Svend Weber

Facing page, Helene Isaksen

Top to bottom: Anne-Sofie between her cousin and uncle. Anne Sofie with mother, 1950. Anne Sofie front right, with family and friends.

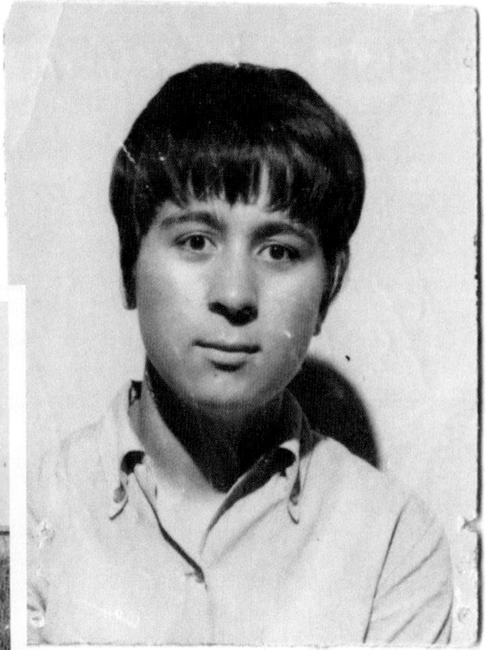

Top to bottom: Anne Sofie, summer 1967. 14 year old Anne Sofie babysitting her cousin. Anne Sofie's mother Helene, center, visitng her future in-laws in 1947.

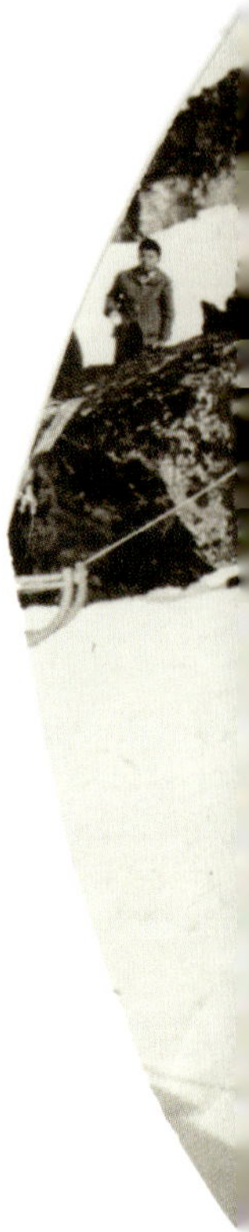

Left to right: Anne Sofie*; On hiking trip to Nuuk, Greenland, spring 1967. With classmates in Helsingor, Denmark. Skiing in Nuuk, 1967. By Soborg Lakeside Bath, July 1966.*

Stof til eftermæle

Mazarine var med i Mitterrands følge

Mitterrands enke Danielle sammen med sønnen Jean-Christophe. Bagved datteren Mazarine og hendes mor Anne Pingeot. Yderst til højre Mitterrands søn Gilbert – Foto: Reuter

Malin Lindgren

– DER GIK ET SUS gennem avisredaktionerne i Storbritannien og USA, da de første billeder fra præsident Mitterrands begravelse tikkede ud af telefoto-maskinerne. I det nærmeste følge sås Danielle Mitterrand flankeret af det afdøde statsoverhoveds tre børn. Parrets to sønner og præsidentens datter med Anne Pingeot, som han havde et fast forhold til. Kunne man bringe de billeder? Ville den professionelle selvcensur ikke få fransk presse til at undgå billeder, der ville give en ridse i Mitterrands perfekte image? De blev bragt i Frankrig, og ingen tog anstød af det.

Tilsvarende billeder ville være en uhørt skandale i Storbritannien og en helt uacceptabel afsløring i USA, hvor politikeres privatliv følges med telelinse, og et enkelt sidespring kan koste en mand både karrieren og omdømmet. Tænk bare den mistænkeliggørelse Clinton, ja selv Bush, har været udsat for. På den baggrund er der noget utroligt befriende ved præsident Mitterrands ønske om, at den 19-årige Mazarine, som fra fødslen fik hans efternavn, skulle følge ham til graven. Hun var hans *fille naturelle*, nturlige datter, det smukke franske ord for det som på andre sprog kaldes uægte eller direkte horebarn. Han var stolt af hende, beskæftigede sig med hende og var få uger før sin død med hende i Ægypten.

Det var ikke en gammel kynikers sidste udfordring til det borgerlige samfund, det

Left to right: Newspaper clipping from January 21, 1996 describing French President Mitterand's funeral which his illegitimate daughter attended without causing any social issues. Drawing from Christmas, 1966 letter from Per, see page 53. Envelope containing letter from Anne Sofie to her brother Per.

3-12-67.

mit værelse.

Nr. 2.

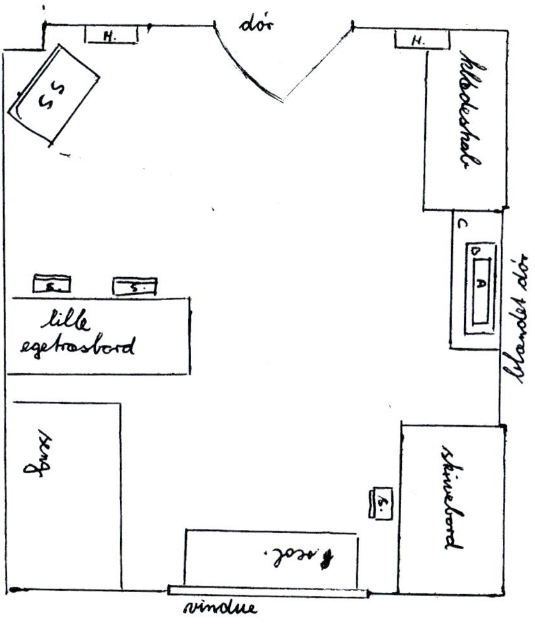

a = båndoptager, b = radio, ~~ok~~ c = grammofonskab, ss = lænestol, s = stol, h = højtalerkasser som sidder på væggen med tre højtalere ~~ok~~ i hver kasse altså 6 højtalere på væggen ialt.

◎ Nuuk
January 9, 1969

Dear Aunt Ruth,

Many thanks for your letter, it was wonderful hearing from you again. We are happy to hear you are going home in August because we would very much like to see you, we miss you a lot. We look forward to showing you our future child. We are looking forward to having the child in this world next month and hope that everything will go as expected. When I saw the midwife on December 17th she said that the child was turning the wrong way and said that they would try turning the child the right way. When I came back 3 weeks later on January 3, the midwife was not there, only two students who examined me. They said that the child was turning the right way, but I think I can feel the child's head right under my chest. I am considering going back to see the midwife and get another exam so I can be certain that it is turning the right way. Arne's mother is looking so much forward to becoming a grandmother. She is a mother to me, she always gives me advice. I am very happy to have her.

Yes, you can save the letters until we meet again. We have also decided to save 10,000-15,000 and then spend the money I receive from the inheritance. You can easily send a check from the Handelsbanken (The Merchants Bank) to Greenland. You can send it to the Grønlandsbanken (Greenland Bank) to my bank account no. xxxxxx.

Yes, thank you, we have had a wonderful Christmas with Arne's parents. We spent the 24th with them and had turkey and that was the first time I tasted it. It was wonderful because Arne's mother is a very good cook. The 25th we spent with my other aunt and we had a big Christmas lunch, it was very nice. For New Year's we had dinner with the in-law's, fired rockets and afterwards drank champagne toasts to

Left to right: Anne Sofie. Grandmother Mariane (mother's mother). Grandparents Hedvig & Josef Weber (father's parents). Anne Sofie, Grandmother Hedvig and Aunt Ruth in Odense, 1967.

Facing page, top to bottom: Anne Sofie with brother Per, September 2005 in Nuuk. Anne Sofie's mother Helene, at her 75th birthday. This page: Pia Christensen Bang, Anne Sofie Hardenberg.

længes ogsaa ssu efter a
paa dig, om du nu ogsa
mark. Hvornaar du skal
rigtig, nok engang i 1948.
om en anden Stilling, s
aa blive heroppe en Aa
ok ikke før til Efteraa
alt jo er paa 2 Aar. Je
mis Christian, men her m
a Stationen ligger saa
vil gerne have at være,
Moder og Fader. Lærer du
t til Fader, du skal paa
nu. Maaned var jeg paa

While the inheritance case is tried, Anne Sofie is of course affected by the disputes. She is happy, however, that she after all has an especially good relationship with her Aunt Ruth, grandmother, her father's Aunt Grethe and brother Bent and sister-in-law May. Besides, her thoughts naturally evolve more around her unborn child while she is mourning her father and several times imagines how he would have reacted to becoming a grandfather. She is certain that he would be proud and it warms her heart. She is convinced that she is having a boy and at no time does she doubt that his name shall be Svend.

◎ Nuuk
Christmas 1968

Dear Per,

Since Christmas is approaching, I am sending you a little Christmas greeting in the hope that you will respond to my letter this time.

You see, I have been thinking a lot about you, and why you do not responding to my letters.

We have moved into the house as of December 1, have decorated it cozily, and only need to replace his nice furniture with our own which we will gradually be purchasing.

Since Christmas is approaching and the days darken, we are all looking forward to Christmas. This year we have not had a lot of snow but we hope that there will be more before the 24th.

I assume you have finished your first term long ago. How did it go this time? I hope you got some good grades.

As of now, we expect to get married in January before the child is born, we have not set a date yet because we also have to talk to my in-law's about it.

I hope you have been in touch with our aunt as she would be more than delighted to have more contact with her grandchildren so she can feel the joy of being a grandparent.

Now I will wish you and your family are all well during Christmas and wish you a happy New Year.

The most loving greetings from
Anne S. and Arne

◉ Nuuk
Christmas 1968

Dear Aunt Ruth,

I truly hope you have received my previous letter from October because I sent some letters from father as proof. I have received the letter with the little pamphlet about the child, thank you. It is not so important now as the case is closed since Britta has agreed that I am Svend's daughter.

I went to talk to Guldborg Chemnitz 14 days ago. She showed me two different documents regarding the distribution of the inheritance. I shall get the other sheet so I can see it all. I will make sure to send it to you so you too can study it a bit. It says I am to inherit 10,000 DKK. Today Guldborg called and told me that she has received a notification from the Engineer Association's pension fund stating I am to receive 363 DKK every month and which I was supposed to start receiving August 1, 1966. So she said that I will probably get a great deal of money the first time. The approximately 10,000 DKK I will also get monthly, but she does not know how much, but it will help a lot since we need the money.

I have good news for you. We have found a house to live in, we moved in December 1. We have been very busy washing and painting it. It is old-fashioned so we have spent a lot of money on it. Arne has put in a kitchen sink with a drain and then we purchased a gas stove for 800 DKK as the house had a coal stove with cracks in several spots. In the living room there was a kerosene stove. There is a kitchen, hallway, dining room, and bedroom and upstairs there are two rooms that we will not be using as it is too cold but there is plenty space for us downstairs. For now, we are using some of our old nice furniture. We have decorated it quite cozily, you should come visit.

Aunt, Arne's mother has mentioned that we should get married in December when her husband comes back from Denmark and today he has returned, so perhaps we will get married in January or, if that does not happen, then it will be after I deliver the child and perhaps we shall have his christening at the same time. Arne's mother said yesterday that we could get married by the mayor but we want to get married in the church! We will write to you as soon as we have spoken to my in-law's about it. By the way, our house is right across from Arne's parents house so that is very good. They invite us over constantly as we do not have much money left but we soon.

I am still working but I will stop by the first of the year since I cannot do it any longer as I am also working when I return home at night and am exhausted. The last month and a half I need to just relax with knitting baby clothes and I have come quite far with it and have also knitted a lovely sweater for Arne. We have been given a great deal of baby clothes from Arne's father Henning from Amager and they are sending us a bassinet so that we do not need to spend money on that. We have probably paid around 200 kroner for baby clothes. We are looking forward to a birth date around the 22nd of February, it really is exciting to see what it will be. Arne wants a boy and I am happy regardless of it being a girl or a boy. Arne's mother says I will have a girl, she is so kind to me, she always asks me how I am and what the midwife said. I think it will be a boy since there are powerful kicks and movement every day. Apart from that we are doing well and Arne is good, his leg is much better. It can be a month between swellings of his knee so we are happy with the progress but he has lost a lot of weight, he works too hard as he has ever since we were told we could borrow the house. He works constantly.

I never hear from Per. Last time I wrote to him was in October but he is still not responding. Now I have written 3 letters without reply, it has to be Britta who is behind it, I have a feeling. She has not had it her way, as she has fought the past 2½ years—the blood samples are correct, you know. I will end for now. Arne and I will wish you all a very merry Christmas and a happy New Year.

The most loving greetings from Anne S. and Arne
P.S. a greeting from Arne's parents.

the New Year. We have not seen anything of mother since we saw her last in mid-December.

It does not sound good that you are unable to make the staff work properly, oh my, that is known all around the world. It cannot be any fun being the one who has to be on their backs.

We have now organized ourselves very cozily. We have purchased furniture and two Ege rugs and a genuine Polish rug, and we have almost purchased everything for the kitchen. It is expensive to set up house. We got quite a lot of kitchen utensils for Christmas from the in-law's and a hand mixer, we got Arne's mothers old hand mixer because she got a big stand mixer for Christmas. Now we are only waiting for the child. We have purchased all the necessities for a baby, cot and pram we will not purchase until the child has arrived.

I have joyous news for you—Arne and I are getting married on January 25. We are having a civil wedding though we had expected to get married in the church. A week ago we received a notification from the priest which needs to be signed by mother but she refused to sign it as we had expected, so I had to write to the governor to ask if he could sign it. For as I have not yet turned 21, because the law up here demands both parties be 21, if you are not you have to have a parents' signature. If the parents refuse to sign it, the governor can sign it, he has the full authority to do so. Mother was summoned to the governor's office where she also refused to sign it. Now I am sick of her behavior, but I will keep a stiff upper lip. We have to invite them but they will not come, we already know that. Arne's parents will be his best men and for me my other aunt and her husband. We will be 20 if mother comes, otherwise 18. We are having the reception at the in-law's for they have a big house, we can all easily fit. It is sad that mother is behaving that way, you know she was completely out of it the day we were there, started to scream and kick and hit my cousin when he asked her why she is against it. When cousin asked her nicely if she would not want to come see how we live, she gave a strict no!

By the way, Lillepus ("cutie pie") got a very nice romper from his future great-grandmother, you see we call the child in my belly Lillepus, it was Henning who started calling it that.

Now we send you the best wishes for the New Year.

The most loving greetings
From Anne Sofie and Arne

⊚ Nuuk
February 7, 1969

Dear Per,

Thank you for your letter which I have been waiting for for almost 3 months. I think it is so sad to have not even gotten a little Christmas greeting for Big Sister, do you not think so? And even though I cannot get in touch with Little Sister you can at least tell me how she is doing. My husband and I would very much like to hear how things are with you.

We had our wedding on 1.25.69 and it went excellent. We had the reception at my in-law's, only the closest family was present. We got many gifts which we had not at all expected – then I got a vacuum cleaner for my morning gift and I gave Arne a full automatic projector. Dinner set from the in-law's and a coffee set of the same kind from my other aunt. I cannot even mention them all, that is how many there were. Now we do not need anything else for the house, we have also just bought an Atlas refrigerator. It probably will not be long now before Lillepus arrives in this world, next week, preferably 2.14. as it should preferably be on Esther's 21st birthday (Esther is Arne's little sister who is in Næstved at nursing school).

Per, I will tell you that we have not married because of the baby but for love. Of course we look forward to having the child, as do the in-law's, they completely understand and accept it.

Aunt Ruth was supposed to have attended our wedding if she knew about it in time so you can understand that we are upset about that.

Yes, thank you, we had a cozy and peaceful Christmas with the in-law's.We got quite a lot of Christmas presents. Now we have had some snow up here, it fell at the end of the month but unfortunately I cannot ski yet. I have actually been encouraged to become a skiing instructor for girls, unfortunately I cannot, but Arne has become one.

We have heard a lot about Bornholm getting a lot of snow but it melts pretty quickly, I guess, and that must be annoying.

We have planned a 3 week long vacation in August to visit Aunt Ruth, of course first and foremost to show her the baby.We might have the baptism down there because I would like Aunt Ruth to be godmother!

We need to hear Aunt Ruth's thoughts first. It could be that she comes up here instead. I hope there will not be any hindrances for meeting with the rest of our family in August (at a baptism, for example?).We will bring our slides of Greenland, the wedding, and the interior of our house so they can see how we live.

I will end for now and hope you will answer my questions, I have always wondered why you do not answer my questions, and I would like some answers. Feel free to tell your opinions about me if I have written anything you do not like.

The most loving greetings from
Anne Sofie and Arne

◉ Nuuk
Christmas 1969

Dear Per,

It sure has been a long time since we have heard anything from you.

Did you get an apprenticeship? Or how are you really doing? Can you please tell me something about what you are doing at the moment?

I heard that Annette was confirmed in October. I wish her all the best in the future.

Here, the time is running from us. At the moment we are busy making Christmas ornaments. My husband and I are also taking a skiing instructor class so we can teach beginners. My husband is the one who teaches along with someone else. It is very exciting. In March a Norwegian skiing instructor will be teaching us more.

We have had a lot of snow up here and my husband goes out hunting for grouse on his cross-country skis every Sunday. So far he has killed 1 hare, 4 grouse, eiders, and guillemots. If he catches more grouse, we will eat them for Christmas.

Our Svend is becoming a big boy, he is big for his age, it will not be long before he starts walking. He started chit-chatting, you bet he is a fresh little guy full of go. I can send you a picture of him if you like, perhaps you already have seen a picture of him from Aunt Grethe, grandmother, or Aunt Ruth?

I hope you and the rest of the family are well.

I wish you and the family a merry Christmas and a happy New Year.

The most loving greetings from
Anne S., Svend, and Arne

This will be the last letter between the two siblings for the next many years. Their relation drifts apart entirely and just like his younger sister and his mother, Per does not have any contact to the rest of her father's family. However, the tight bond is preserved between Anne Sofie and her Aunt Ruth, who is gradually becoming an integral part of the little family in Greenland. Over the next years, Ruth visits Anne Sofie and Arne several times for both baptisms and confirmations.

◎ Nuuk
February 12, 1970

Dear Aunt Ruth,

Many thanks for your letters. I apologize that you have not heard from us for so long. You see, I started working in the nursery 1½ months ago; a Danish lady I know takes care of Svend. I work form 7:30 AM to 5 PM, 1½ hour lunch break, then we pay 90 kroner for 5 days to have him taken care of, almost half of my pay. You see, there is not room for him in the nursery. He has been so much under the weather since Christmas, we have all had the flu at the same time, it took Svend 2 weeks to recover. I had been vaccinated and only had something wrong with my throat. After the flu, Svend has been more or less sick constantly.

By the way, thank you so much for the Christmas presents and clothes for Svend, they all fit him, except for the pants which were hemmed a little short. He wears them a lot. Christmas went very well – he was calm and temperate and was very impressed with the Christmas tree – he also got a lot of toys. We were home all three of us most of the days enjoying Christmas by ourselves. We had such bad weather during the holiday.

You bet he has grown big and tall, but he lost weight after the flu, and he has become so stubborn. He never wants to sleep in his own bed. He sleeps in ours every night, he climbs over as easy as anything. We have talked about buying another bed that is taller, we have to, we cannot have him sleeping with us. Jacob and Ingrid, some of our best friends, just gave him a sled. It is because Arne stopped smoking 1½ months ago and he and Ingrid bet a pair of ski poles for 60 kroner but Arne already had two, so Ingrid continued smoking and then they finally agreed that it might as well be a sled. You see, they had talked about Arne and him making it, but he did not have a lot of time. We almost never see him on Saturdays and Sundays, he is skiing both days no matter what the weather is. He is attending the Greenlandic Slalom Championship in March, and he will now be training every night. I sure hope he does not break a leg, then it will be difficult for him. I do cross-country and slalom but I do not have a lot of time now. It is sad now that we have had so much snow, so it is difficult getting around.

It will not be long before Svend turns one. I am going to invite the closest family for 9 AM, that is the time he was born, have friends over all day, then potentially inviting family for dinner.

I shall talk to Arne about sending you an 8mm film of Svend so you can see him and how he has developed. You see, Arne has bought an 8mm camera so he can shoot him, that was really expensive but because he stopped smoking, it is really good. We have slides from Christmas too. By the way, he got kamik boots for Christmas from our other aunt and a timiak, a sort of Greenlandic jacket. The kamik boots were a little too small so he got some new ones from grandmother for his birthday.

We are happy to hear you enjoyed the Christmas parcel and that you visit Peter, they are very pleased with that. At the moment Arne's father is hospitalized at Sana.

It seems Britta is coming to her senses. It is lovely that she has told Annette the story, I wonder how she reacted? I think too it is silly of her to cut her contact to father's family and try to get the kids away from them. Let us now hope for the good side and the chance to meet them both so we can enjoy each other.

If you wish, we can send you salmon and reindeer or lamb meat, just write what you prefer and we will send it.

Apart from that, we are doing well at the moment. Would you not want to come up here and work for a year at the new health care assistant school? Or at the hospital, it would be wonderful if that is possible.

I will end for now. Arne and Svend send all their greetings.

The most loving greetings from all three of us.

the bay and the seals arrived.What do you think? Arne actually shot a big seal on Sunday but he did not catch it. He watched while it slowly disappeared in the deep, for he did not have a hook to grab it with.You have no idea how frustrating that was.

Over the weekend he is going out in the umiaaraq (fishing boat) to shoot eiders or seagulls.

Otherwise we are doing well apart from Arne being so sick because of the unstable weather we have this year. I hope he will not be too sick in Denmark, he can, of course, not help it.

Peter is doing well, he is very happy to get home again.

Aunt, I will finish for now, be well and say hi to aunt and Aunt Grethe and Ellen Margrethe.

The most loving greetings
from Svend, Arne, and Anne Sofie

So the little family goes on vacation in Denmark, especially to partake in Anne Sofie's grandmother's 80th birthday in Odense. Here, they are looking very much forward to seeing the entire family on her father's side and to showing them little Svend for the first time. However, neither Anne Sofie's siblings nor their mother show up for that occasion and it disappoints her, she feels bad for her aunt because they stay away. Anne Sofie is, however, pleased with the family's excitement about Svend and tells them at the same time that she is pregnant again and expecting her and Arne's second child in December that same year.

On December 9, 1970, Anne Sofie delivers her second son who is baptized Jesper. Arne works in a skiing association and the following year he applies to a position as a traffic recruit with Grønlandsfly (airline) and is accepted. The Hardenbergs are stationed first in Paamiut and then in Qasigiannguit where they live for about five years and have another son, Arne Junior, in 1973.

While they live in Qasigiannguit, Arne initiates the founding of a cable tv association. The first image on the tape machine appears December 31, 1973 – a great experience for everyone. Anne Sofie and Arne have a studio in their dining room and Anne Sofie takes care of the shows in the evening and makes abstracts in Greenlandic. The two also take part in the founding of the skiing club during that time.

Anne Sofie's plans for education are postponed indefinitely and she takes many different jobs during those years, including temporary teacher/interpreter, in a daycare center, in a fish factory, and in the radio house. When the family moves back to Nuuk in *when the children come, we shall see who is the best – but it is something that is good for all muscles and I can feel that I am very comfortable with it. The chiropractor has also promised now that this year it will start going in the right direction.*

Today I spoke with the secretary at Birkerød state school. She will send me some information about the school which I will then pass on to you and I was supposed to go see the school afterwards. They were not too happy about it though because the children were not to be disturbed during class – but I told them that I did not need to, I just wanted to get an impression of the school, etc. From an acquaintance who has lived in Birkerød for many years, I have heard that the school is very well renowned and several who have had their children there have been very satisfied.

Yes, it is true that your father would have turned 65 on the 19th of this month. I thought about it too even though it is hard to imagine your father as a semi-old man. He lives on in you – and it is my great comfort that you are doing so well and that your children have so many of his good qualities – he was a man of peace – and I have probably in my younger days often been a little brute in my statements when it came to things I was unsatisfied with – but then he would always be the one to even things out. You were never to talk unfavorably about anyone when he was present.

I had Reverend Vick's old housekeeper with me for New Year's Eve – she is over 80 but manages pretty well. We actually had a falling out before she left – I showed her some pictures from the trip to Greenland but then she started criticizing Denmark's relationship to Greenland – and then I got angry – and it ended with her leaving a little sooner than planned. That is her own fault when she cannot behave properly.

Yes, it is strange that Svend is going to school where you were as a young girl – but life is of course so peculiar at times. I can send you regards from Michael, who wrote to me for Christmas, that he has taken the doctorate degree in history with his dissertation on Louisiana under the French reign. He just left for Brazil as a ship priest on a luxury steamboat but I know that he will very much like to visit Greenland. Whether he will make it is uncertain, he turns 77 this year!!!

I think it is wonderful that Svend and Klaus will be together and you can tell Klaus that he, too, is always welcome with Svend.

Now I shall wish you a happy spring with your studies. I am sure it must be nice to think that you will then be all done and it is also good that you are happy with your job. I assume you have read about the Kronebank scandal back home? It will be an expensive deal for the country. We never thought something like that could happen in Denmark, it is unbelievable.

Now I hope you are all doing well. I have invited Bent and May over for Greenlandic food in the near future.

Loving greetings to you all,
Aunt Ruth

◎ April 9, 1985

Dear Anne Sofie and Arne,

This will be a post-Easter greeting. As you have probably felt too, we have had a sad time because of all kinds of strikes before Easter. The Prime Minister has encouraged normalizing conditions in the country again – it is too expensive in all ways to have old people sitting without heat and no transportation for several days. Unfortunately it seems like it has not ended entirely – there are of course always people who have to make trouble. We do not have petrol in Copenhagen – at least not where I do my shopping – bicycles are not patched – and all cabs are driving – those that use petrol can see an end to it but fortunately there are many using diesel.

Henning called me the other day to wish me happy Easter – that sure was nice of him – I think he was spending it with his sister. He told me that he sometimes got very dizzy when walking on the street – he thinks he got lead poisoning up in Greenland – but the doctors will not believe him. They say he smokes too much. So it is not entirely good with him. I have started again after my broken ribs – now I hope it will work but the back is not entirely fixed yet.

I am working during Easter. Now spring has arrived, it is really lovely after all that snow this year, but April 1st we had another good layer of melting snow.

Jonathan Motzfeldt was on TV the other day. They showed him in the USA where he was received quite nobly. I think that was before they had gone on strike on TV because they stopped working, too, just like the telephone and mail services. Otherwise there is nothing new – Bent came over for lunch the other day – the chairman of the organization for salaried employees had sent them to the street –

if they did not want to demonstrate in front of Christiansborg. It is a good thing he knows the way things are here. He does not know yet whether he wants to switch jobs – because the new one is in a union – and he is of course not interested in all the issues with strikes – which undoubtedly will ensue there too – so he is a little wary.

Now I hope you are all well – I am sure you are busy studying – but hopefully Arne has had some time off during Easter so you have all been able to get out skiing together.

Anne Lise is busy studying – it is over soon, then we shall see what she wants. You see, she thinks she can get in to all the university schools but whether the municipality will keep paying for her is another matter. She will probably discover the realities of life when the time comes.

Be well now – loving greetings to you all.
Aunt Ruth

The years go by and Anne Sofie continues to confide in her Aunt Ruth about big and small things through letters, phone conversations, and visits.

Over time, Anne Sofie and Arne's marriage breaks up. Anne Sofie feels lonely, insecure, and unhappy but fights to hold the days together. The children grow up and move away from home and when Aunt Ruth at the end of 2001, falls ill and dies, Anne Sofie makes a drastic decision.

It is November 2001, and it is a wet cold fall in Copenhagen when Anne Sofie arrives with the plane from Greenland and rushes to the *Rigshospitalet* (hospital in Copenhagen). Here, Aunt Ruth lies sick, weak, and well aware that her time is running out. She has sent for her niece whom she long ago made her heiress. She is obviously happy to have Anne Sofie present and, partly sedated, she starts talking about Britta, her sister-in-law, whom she has neither seen nor spoken with for several years. Anne Sofie has no idea what to do but she senses that her aunt would like to get in touch with Britta and her children, Per and Annette. Therefore, she starts searching for her half-siblings the following day and finds several people in the phonebook called Annette Weber. She calls them all starting at the top and quickly gets one. Anne Sofie explains that their mutual aunt is on her deathbed at *Rigshospitalet* but the sister refuses to visit her because she has not had any contact with Aunt Ruth for many years. However, she promises to tell her mother about the situation. Anne Sofie also gets a phone number for her brother Per but he, too, refuses to visit Ruth. The old aunt passes away a few days later without seeing her brother's two youngest children and their mother.

Anne Sofie is alone at the final goodbye with her beloved aunt in the hospital's chapel where she sings Greenlandic psalms to her and prays the Lord's Prayer. Arne is also in Copenhagen but the separated couple have over the past years distanced themselves from each other and Arne later explains to Anne Sofie that he thought she preferred being alone in that difficult and very private moment. To Anne Sofie it is a definitive moment in which she realizes that their marriage truly is over and she must move on alone. It will be several months, however, before the decision about moving out and getting a divorce is realized.

After the funeral, Anne Sofie has contacted her sister again and the two meet alone for the first time at a restaurant in Copenhagen. Here they talk through many childhood experiences and, not least, traumas and lies, and Annette hears Anne Sofie's version of everything that has transpired. After that, Anne Sofie also meets with her brother and the three siblings slowly start nurturing a new contact with each other through letters, mails, and phone conversations.

Three months after Aunt Ruth's funeral, Anne Sofie finally tells Arne that she wishes to get a divorce. He is unhappy but accepts her decision. Several months pass, however, before she actually moves out of their mutual home, partly because she only then has somewhere to move to, namely when she is hired as a consumer consultant and gets staff residence. By the end of August 2002, the divorce is a reality.

Anne Sofie was in Denmark again that same summer, this time to surprise Per with a visit on his 50th birthday. He is having a party for his family and friends in his home in Rudkøbing on Langeland and is happy when his big sister from Greenland suddenly shows up and he proudly introduces her to the family, including his oldest son, who meets Anne Sofie for the first time.

The following couple of years of Anne Sofie's life is filled with intense self-development. She seeks help from a clairvoyant and reads stacks of books about personal development. She visits several alternative practitioners and slowly but surely she becomes stronger and stronger. At one time in the beginning of the process she also has quite a few physical disorders and for a while had a hard time walking. She seeks out a reflexologist who tells her that it is simply because she has so many tears and so much anger piled up in her body. Gradually, Anne Sofie finds a balance with herself and starts a new eventful chapter of her life.

Not until this moment does she finally find peace in her relationship with Helene. At Helene's 75th birthday in 2002, Anne Sofie calls her *Mother* for the first time and gives a speech about forgiveness and love.

In 2004 Anne Sofie decides, after being inspired by a Saami woman, to establish herself as an independent cook. She writes recipe books, cooks at big events, and ladles out her enormous knowledge about Greenlandic resources. Alongside this, she also becomes a cab operator and hires her two youngest sons as drivers and is officially appointed Nordic food ambassador. She attends several slow food fairs and has lots of experience sharing information with Saami women and other Nordic cooks. Most recently she founded the company Kvann LLC with three other entrepreneurs for the sale and refinement of Greenlandic herbs, not least angelica, which she considers to be the crown jewel among Greenlandic plants.

◉ September 2009

Dear Mother,

Many years have passed since the letters in this book have been written. I have felt it has been important to tell the story about the losses I experienced in my childhood: the loss of you because you had to travel to the tuberculosis station in Denmark – and the loss of my father whom I did not know when I was a child.

There have been many reasons for our relationship to have been bad.

When I read my letters over, I recognize the feelings I had then. But now that I am older and since my divorce I have spent several years healing myself, I can now also look at my former life with new and clear eyes.

I can understand that your reluctance for me contacting my family in Denmark was also about protecting me against disappointments, and I can see that I have been hard on you and that I was not the only one who had a tough life.

I can also understand and forgive that your way of reacting to my choices in life have been based on a conviction on what was best for me.

All parents of course wish the best for their children – but it is also important to understand that the children cannot always use the parents good advice but have to make their own decisions.

Today I am proud of having grown up with my Grandmother Mariane whom I have much to thank for. My childhood home was always clean even though she had had many children to raise and was widowed early on. It has given me the foundation and life strength I have today.

I would like to thank you, Mom, for being born and for feeling like a citizen of the world in my current life. I love you and am happy that we today have a good relationship to each other. Hopefully we can live together for many years to come.You are still a beautiful and fresh woman for your 82 years. I am proud of you and you are a good example to other people.

While I wrote this letter I stopped many times because tears were streaming. It is always difficult writing feelings on a piece of paper because we never talked about it with each other. I now feel a great relief in body, soul, and heart after writing to you.

Your precious daughter,
Anne Sofie

Anne Sofie Hardenberg originally trained as a bank clerk but has in recent years made her great interest for and knowledge about Greenlandic food into her main occupation. She is a writer of the recipe book *Igaassat – Recipes*, Atuakkiorfik, 2007, which came in third in an international competition for cook books. The same year, she was appointed Greenland's ambassador for New Nordic Food and in 2008 she started the company *Kvann LLC* with three partners in Denmark.

Pia Christensen Bang is trained as a journalist and has lived and worked in Greenland for a number of years. From 2005-2007 she was employed as news director at KNR, Greenland Radio, and from 2008 she was communication employee for Air Greenland. She has previously written the book *Tough Women*, containing seven biographies of Greenlandic women, milik publishing, 2007.

Routledge Revivals

The Introduction to Hegel's Philosophy of Fine Art

Originally published in 1905, Bosanquet's translation of Hegel's *Philosophy of Fine Art* brings Hegel's commentary and analysis of what constitutes beauty and fine art to an English audience as well as presenting his own viewpoints on the work and what is at the heart of true philosophical theory. This title will be of interest to students of philosophy and art.